and Margaret, upon her return, was herself imprisoned for opening a clinic and freely giving birth control advice.

Yet throughout those turbulent years, Margaret never stopped lecturing, writing, arranging conferences, and arousing the public conscience in any way she could. And at last her dream came true: The birth control movement became worldwide, and Margaret Sanger is honored as its founder.

Vivian Werner's well-researched biography, highlighted by relevant photographs, is as dramatic as was the life of its remarkable subject.

Margaret Sanger:
WOMAN REBEL

By VIVIAN WERNER
Illustrated with photographs

Margaret Sanger:
WOMAN REBEL

HAWTHORN BOOKS, INC.   PUBLISHERS   NEW YORK

First Edition: 1970

Designed by Terry Reid

For my sister, Ruth

CONTENTS

Margaret Sanger:
WOMAN REBEL

Chapter **1**

"CHILD OF THE DEVIL"

THE FAMILY WAS POOR; there was no doubt about that. This year there wouldn't even be any presents for Christmas.

Not that Michael and Annie Higgins had ever had money for luxuries. Still, the year before, when Margaret was seven, she had found an orange and an apple in her Christmas stocking. There had been a warm coat for one of the older boys as well, and sturdy shoes for another. Now, though, they could count themselves lucky if the stew for dinner could be stretched to provide second helpings.

Margaret, remembering the apple and the orange, stared

glumly out the window. From it she could see the shabby houses of the workers clustered around the church.

The church! There would be gifts there! Why hadn't she thought of it? She pulled on her coat and darted out the door.

At the church a crowd of children waited impatiently for the priest to hand out the tissue-wrapped gloves and scarves piled under the tree. Margaret joined the line, inching forward with the others. At last she stood before Father Coghlan.

"Merry Christmas," he boomed, holding out a package. As Margaret reached for it, Father Coghlan looked down. "Oh, ho! You're a Higgins, aren't ye?" he asked. Before Margaret could speak, he snatched the gift away. "There's nothing for ye here," he said. "Be off with ye, now."

At once the other children began to howl. "Child of the Devil!" they screamed. "Child of the Devil!"

Margaret turned and ran. All the way home, the words rang in her ears. Yet her heart swelled with pride in the "Devil"—her father.

The Devil? Because his beliefs were not those of the others? The Devil? Because he was not afraid to speak up?

The Devil? He had hated slavery so much he had run away from home when he was only fifteen to enlist in the Union Army and fight in the Civil War. He'd been wounded—yes, and decorated for bravery, too.

Margaret's father had hardly been discharged from the army before he married Anne Purcell, whose own Irish ancestry showed in her milk-white skin and her abundant black hair. The young couple set up housekeeping in the grimy industrial city of Corning, New York. Then, as now, it was known for the manufacture of glass.

Higgins, though, earned his living carving tombstones. The

saints and angels he chiseled were the most beautiful for miles around. But it was a wonder he got any work done.

His workshop was filled with visitors from morning until night. All came to hear Michael Higgins discuss politics or economics or thunder against bigotry in his lilting Irish brogue.

He didn't believe in private property and was the only Socialist in Corning. He had contempt for the Church, yet defended the right of everyone to worship as he pleased. Just as stoutly, he defended the rights of nonbelievers to be heard.

One of Higgins's heroes was Colonel Robert Ingersoll. He was an agnostic, who wasn't sure of the existence of God and demanded some clear proof of it before he would believe in Him. Higgins admired him so much that he invited Ingersoll to speak in Corning.

When "Colonel Bob" accepted, Higgins rented the only hall in town for the event. Since it belonged to the Catholic Church, he was careful to keep the name of the speaker a secret from Father Coghlan.

He did, too, until just before meeting time. Then the news reached the priest. Father Coghlan, his face red with rage, at once ordered the hall locked and barred. It made no difference that a crowd had already gathered; everyone was to be kept out.

Many people there really wanted to hear Ingersoll. But many others had come in a surly mood. Within a short time, tempers on both sides flared, and clashes broke out.

Thereupon Higgins took charge. The meeting, he announced, would be held in the open, in a nearby woods. Those who wished to hear Ingersoll were invited to follow him. Then he put his arm around Ingersoll's shoulder, and the two—with Margaret at their heels—marched off.

The procession had gone only a short way when a tomato

sailed through the air, landing on Higgins's shirt. Then a rotten egg splattered on Ingersoll. In a moment there was flying garbage everywhere.

Still Higgins and Ingersoll strode on, their heads high. Ingersoll spoke more eloquently than ever, as if to show that no howling mob would stop them!

But Father Coghlan made life miserable for Higgins and his family from then on. He considered Higgins his mortal enemy and urged all in the parish to shun him "like the Devil himself." Above all, he insisted that they go elsewhere for their gravestones.

Soon, Higgins's earnings fell off. Then they vanished altogether, while the Higgins family continued to grow.

There were already five children in the household when Margaret was born, in Corning, on September 12, 1879. Five others came later. All were hale and hearty, and Annie Higgins often boasted that "not one was born with a blotch or a blemish."

She herself was a frail woman, who had frequent coughing fits. Yet she was tireless in the care of her children. She cleaned and cooked and marketed. She patched and darned, bending over her needle until late at night. She washed and ironed, seeing to it that Higgins had a spotless, beautifully starched and pressed white shirt each day, no matter what *she* wore.

Higgins? He was the most impractical of men. Send him to the store for a dozen bananas and he was likely to buy *fifteen* dozen, grandly handing them out to the neighborhood children while his own went without. One day he arrived home, looking like the Pied Piper of Hamelin, followed by a ragged horde of eight small children. Their mother, he explained to Annie, had typhoid fever, and there was no one at home to care for the little tykes. So, for two long months, Annie Higgins cared for

Top (left): Anne Purcell Higgins, mother of Margaret Sanger; (right):
Michael Hennessy Higgins, father of Margaret Sanger. Bottom (left):
Margaret Higgins, 1894; (right): The Higgins sisters, clockwise from
top: Nan, Mary, Ethel, and Margaret.

all eight of them, in addition to her own—and without a word of complaint.

But, then, Annie never did complain. While her husband had his head in the clouds, Annie kept her feet planted firmly on the ground and accepted most of the responsibility for the family. If a child was unfairly punished at school, Annie marched off to give the teacher a piece of her mind. If a tramp crept into the house to sleep—Higgins didn't believe in locking doors—Annie took her broom and chased him away, while Higgins continued to read his book of poetry or philosophy.

It was only in medical matters that Anne Higgins got any help from her husband. He served as the family doctor, curing almost everything with a strong dose of "good Irish whiskey." He set bones and lanced boils and delivered the babies who arrived with such regularity.

The children were far more dependable. They got up early and did their chores before the five-mile walk to school. The girls set the table and dressed the younger ones; the boys fed the chickens and milked the cow. In the evening there were other chores before homework and bed.

There was no time for play except during vacations. Then the Higgins brood made up for lost time. They hiked in the woods or hunted. In winter they skated on the pond. When there was snow on the ground, they bundled up in blankets and piled into the sleigh to ride behind their bony old horse.

In summer they played baseball or went swimming. Best of all, they put on plays in the barn. That was when Margaret took charge, casting the others in whatever role she thought suitable. "Bob, you be the wolf," she directed. "Henry, you be the bear." She, of course, was the star, thrilling to the applause of the small audience at the end of each act.

Vacation was a time for reading, too. Margaret, like the others, was encouraged to browse through Michael Higgins's library—for all his poverty, it was one of the best in Corning —and to study the thick volumes there. Most of them were books on economics or political theory. Margaret found them dull.

Higgins, however, insisted that such books would "elevate the mind." Margaret brought home novels from the public library, which her father had fought to establish. She liked romantic adventure stories like *The Count of Monte Cristo* or *The Three Musketeers,* but her father called them trash. Nonetheless, he always permitted Margaret to read them. What else could he do, when he took such pride in opposing censorship?

The children were encouraged to speak their minds, too, although most others, in those days, were expected to be seen and not heard. Moreover, Higgins insisted that they think for themselves, as Margaret learned while she was still very young.

Higgins had come upon her as she knelt, reciting a prayer Annie had taught her: "Give us this day our daily bread . . ."

"What's that you're saying?" he asked.

Margaret looked up, surprised. Surely he knew! Still, she answered, "Why, that's the Lord's Prayer."

"Who were you speaking to?" Higgins went on.

"Why, to God!"

"Is God a baker?"

Margaret was confused for a moment. Then she thought of an explanation. "No, of course God is not a baker, but He creates the rain, the sunshine, and all the things that make the wheat grow."

"Well, so that's the idea," Higgins said with a chuckle. "Wouldn't it be better to say what you mean?"

From then on, Margaret said what she meant. She also meant what she said, as the family found out in due time.

Margaret was sixteen when someone gave her the first pair of kid gloves she had ever owned. She pulled them on one morning, on her way to the local high school, pausing now and then to smooth the fingers. When she arrived at the school yard, the bell for class had already rung.

Margaret rushed to her room and, breathless, sank into her seat. Just then, her teacher—a sour-faced spinster—looked up. "Ah, your ladyship," she sneered. "So you've decided to honor us with your presence!"

Margaret picked up her books and slammed her desk shut. Then, without a word, she stormed out.

At home she announced she would never go back. "I'd rather go to jail," she declared.

First Higgins, and then Nan and Mary, her older sisters, pleaded with Margaret to listen to reason, to change her mind. Without an education, they pointed out, she would have to spend the rest of her life working in a factory. Could anything be worse than that?

Yes! Going back to *that* school could be, Margaret assured them.

Finally Nan and Mary, as they so often did, solved the problem. Margaret would go to Claverack College, about fifty miles away. A scholarship could be arranged to pay for her tuition. Nan and Mary would buy the books and clothes she needed while Margaret worked for her room and board.

That fall, Margaret packed her small suitcase. At the station she kissed each and everyone good-bye, then boarded the train. As it pulled out of the station, Annie Higgins's eyes were wet.

But Margaret's were shining. Corning lay behind her and a new world was ahead.

Chapter **2**

THAT NEW WORLD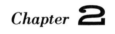

WHO COULD HAVE asked for anything more than Claverack?

Not Margaret, certainly.

All her teachers seemed fascinating, broad-minded, alert. The campus was beautiful; from it one could see the broad sweep of the Hudson River.

There were boys at Claverack, but Margaret paid little attention to them. She was too busy making friends with girls like Esther Farquharson and Amelia Stuart. They came from New York, wore fashionable clothes, and went to hit plays as casually as Margaret went to the corner grocery store.

The other girls were as impressed with Margaret as she was with them. They listened spellbound as she argued for women's rights, for an end to child labor, for any of the social reforms her father supported.

One day Esther took Margaret aside. "You'll never get a beau," she warned, "if you talk like that."

"Why not?" Margaret asked, scarcely able to believe her ears.

"You know what boys are like," Esther explained. "*They* want girls to leave the thinking up to them!"

"But I'm just as intelligent as any boy!"

Esther laughed. "Of course. But you mustn't let *them* know it."

Margaret merely shrugged. What did she care? She had no intention of marrying, anyway. There were more important things to do, like becoming an actress.

Years before, in Corning, a touring company had given a performance of *Uncle Tom's Cabin*. Margaret hadn't had the ten cents she needed to buy a ticket. Still, she managed to slip into the theater and see the play. From that moment on she dreamed of seeing her name in lights.

The teachers at Claverack were certain that Margaret could be a great actress. When several urged her to apply for a role in a new play, she wrote to the producer. He replied at once, asking Margaret for the measurement of her calves and ankles!

She was furious and tore the letter to shreds. If theatrical producers were interested in the shape of her legs, instead of her acting ability, she wanted nothing to do with them. She would be a doctor instead, she decided. Medicine, after all, was a dignified profession.

After Claverack she planned to go to Cornell. Her grades were excellent; in spite of the time taken up by waiting on table, she found some for student activities, too. That would help her to get a scholarship. Already, she saw herself, doctor's satchel in hand, as she cured the sick and healed the wounded.

Then the letter came from Michael Higgins. Annie was desperately ill, he wrote. Margaret was needed at home to care for her.

She took the next train to Corning, where her father was waiting at the station. His sober face told Margaret the truth at once: her mother had only a short while to live. The coughing spells that had racked her body for so many years had grown far worse. Annie was now so weak that she could not walk and had to be carried from room to room in Higgins's strong arms. Within a few months, she died of tuberculosis.

Without Annie, Higgins was as helpless as a baby. Really, though, hadn't he always been? Margaret still did—would always—applaud his stand for liberty and admire his radical views. But now she saw them as a luxury, paid for with Annie's life.

Nan and Mary had left Corning to go to work, so it was up to Margaret and her younger sister, Ethel, to take charge. Margaret was the one to manage the family finances. Just as her mother had, she struggled to make ends meet. But no matter how she tried, Higgins found fault with her.

Without Annie to wait on him hand and foot, he grew harsh and bitter. He no longer talked to the children or listened to them. Often he flew into a rage when the girls entertained their beaux on the front porch and would order them, in no uncertain terms, to leave..

Secretly, Margaret was glad to see them go. To her, all the young men of Corning were dullards. Who would want to marry one of them? Who would want the kind of life that Annie had led, with its constant, back-breaking work? Without money? And with babies coming all the time?

Marry a boy from Corning? No, thank you!

At last, the Easter Margaret was twenty, she was able to escape the local boys and her father. She went to New York, then, to spend the holiday with her Claverack friend, Esther Farquharson. Before long, Margaret had blurted out her story.

Esther spoke to her mother, who suggested that Margaret take up nursing. That would give her independence. There was even a hospital nearby, at Westchester, where Margaret might be accepted at once for training. Mrs. Farquharson knew the director there; she would call and make the arrangements.

She was true to her word; a few weeks later Margaret entered Westchester County Hospital as a student nurse. She spent three years there and was then ready for further work at Manhattan Eye and Ear Hospital in the very heart of New York City.

Compared to Westchester, Manhattan Hospital was paradise. All the equipment was new; the nursing staff enjoyed the most modern conveniences. No longer need Margaret run up and down three flights of stairs to fetch medicine or tend a patient. There were plenty of elevators at Manhattan, and a large enough staff to care for all the sick. There were even special pans to sterilize instruments, instead of tin laundry tubs like those at Westchester.

There, Margaret had often begun her rounds at dawn. At times she worked through the night, then fell into bed too tired to take her clothes off. Even when she developed tubercular glands and underwent an operation for them, she was allowed only three weeks to recuperate. Then she was back at work once more from morning till night. But at Manhattan, there was plenty of time to rest, and time for recreation, too.

One night, at a dance for the staff, a doctor introduced Margaret to William Sanger. He was a young architect who had brought along the plans for a house he was designing for the doctor. Sanger spread his blueprints out on a table in the reception room, and the doctor, Margaret, and he studied them carefully.

Except for the way he kept his intense dark eyes fastened constantly on Margaret, there seemed nothing unusual about Sanger. After he rolled up his blueprints and left, Margaret forgot all about him as she whirled around the dance floor in the arms of the doctor.

She was amazed, therefore, to find Sanger waiting for her, early the next morning, as she went for her usual walk. It was only seven thirty! Surely Sanger hadn't been waiting for her all night!

Before Margaret could speak, Sanger greeted her. "Good morning, Miss Higgins. May I join you in your walk?"

Margaret could hardly refuse. "Why, of course," she said as Sanger fell into step beside her.

The next morning Bill Sanger again waited for Margaret. He did so the following day, too, and every morning for almost six months.

Day after day they strode through the still-deserted streets, while Bill talked of the future. He was already putting money in a savings bank. One day there would be enough to go to Paris. Then he could give up architecture for painting. His face glowed as he spoke of the studio he would find in Montparnasse, or perhaps Montmartre, and of the artists there who were just becoming known in America. And Margaret? Margaret would go with him. Of course, she would!

Bill's house plans were models of careful drawing, but his

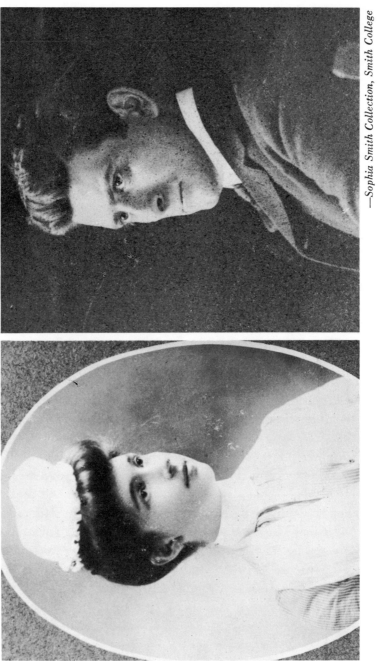

Left: Margaret Sanger as a student nurse; right: Bill Sanger.

own actions were most often decided on the spur of the moment. Seeing a scarf or a handbag he liked, he would buy it for Margaret without a second thought. If he read an announcement of an opera or a play he thought she might enjoy, he immediately bought tickets. To Margaret, who had had to count every penny, this was a whole new world.

Bill often spoke of life with Margaret, but he never actually asked her to marry him. Instead, one afternoon, he suggested a ride in the country. Once on the way, he suggested they stop at the home of a minister, a friend of his.

There Margaret found that Bill had arranged everything. The minister was prepared for a ceremony, the witnesses were waiting. Bill had the ring and the marriage license in his pocket. There was even a supply of rice on hand!

After their wedding that August day in 1902, Mr. and Mrs. William Sanger lived in a tiny apartment while they built their castles in the air. All that Bill had dreamed of was to be theirs —fame, fortune, and above all, Paris.

In a few months, though, all came tumbling down. Margaret was not well; when she consulted a doctor, she learned that she had the beginnings of tuberculosis. He urged her to go west.

But Margaret was already expecting their first baby. How could she leave Bill at such a time? Instead, she decided to enter a sanatorium in the Adirondacks. As soon as possible, Bill joined her there.

The Sangers returned to New York when the baby was due. Bill saw to it that Margaret would get the best of care by sending her to one of the city's leading obstetricians. To make doubly sure, she was sent to see another doctor, just as well known, who would handle the case if the first could not be reached.

But the night the baby was born, *both* doctors were attending other women! The frantic Bill rushed around the neighborhood until he found a young man, just out of medical school, who delivered the baby. Because he had had so little experience, Margaret suffered through the entire night. But the baby—a little boy they named Stuart, for Amelia Stuart who had been Margaret's friend at Claverack—was born without "a blotch or a blemish" like the Higgins children before him.

When Margaret was well enough, the family, with a nurse to care for Stuart, returned to the small house they had taken in the Adirondacks. At first Margaret helped the nurse, bathing Stuart herself or feeding him. But soon she was too ill to leave her bed. She lay there for months, following the orders of the famous Dr. Trudeau, one of the country's greatest experts on tuberculosis, to swallow a quart of creosote and a dozen eggs each day.

Bill could no longer stay with Margaret. His savings, which had been intended for a studio in Paris, had long since been used up to pay doctors and hospitals. Now he was forced to borrow for daily expenses. To pay off his debts, he went back to New York, where he could find work.

One day several of Dr. Trudeau's assistants gathered at Margaret's bedside, urging her to go back to the sanatorium. Margaret said nothing; it hardly mattered. They began to ask about the care of Stuart. "Do you want your brother to care for him?"

"I don't care."

"Your mother-in-law? Your sister? Who?"

Margaret's answer was always the same. "I don't care."

Finally the doctors filed out of the room. Only the youngest stayed. "Don't be like this, Mrs. Sanger," he said gently. "Do something! Want something! Otherwise, you'll never get well."

That night, lying wide awake, Margaret understood what the young doctor was saying. Everyone thought she was dying!

Before dawn, her mind was made up. She would go to New York.

She called the nurse and told her to dress Stuart. She sent for a car and was driven to the station. Before she boarded the train, she sent a telegram to Bill.

He was waiting for her at Grand Central Station. Margaret rushed to him, afraid he would order her back to the mountains. She tried to explain to him why she had come back, her words tumbling out in a rush. "I don't want to die, Bill. I don't want to die."

Bill put his arm around her, calm, gentle, tender as always. "You did just right, Margaret," he said. "You won't die. *I* won't let you die."

Chapter **3**

BACK TO HEALTH—BACK TO WORK

MARGARET WAS UNDER a doctor's care for another year, as she fought her way back to health. For a few months the Sanger family lived in a small hotel. But soon Margaret was well enough to look for the place in the country that she and Bill were willing to settle for, since they couldn't have Paris.

They found what they wanted at Hastings-on-Hudson, where a community of teachers, doctors, lawyers, and a few artists had sprung up. The two bought a plot of land overlooking the river and moved into a rented cottage while their own house was being built.

Bill himself drew the plans for their house. It was to have

everything they wanted—a broad porch with a magnificent view, a paneled library, a studio in which Bill could paint, and a large nursery for Stuart and the other children they hoped for.

Bill supervised the building of the house. Often, he and Margaret worked on it themselves. They stained the woodwork, and they painted the kitchen. Together, they constructed the window of leaded panes to be set at the top of the hall stairs.

Margaret was blissfully happy. Just running the house and caring for Stuart was all she wanted. Later, she enjoyed going with the other women to New York to shop or to see a matinee. She joined the local literary club, too, where the ladies of Hastings regularly discussed a Victorian novel or even a work of Shakespeare.

But as time passed, Margaret grew restless. The world she lived in was hardly real. Her perfect little house might have been *A Doll's House*, the title of a play by Henrik Ibsen that everyone was then talking about; her life might have been that of Ibsen's heroine, Nora.

Why waste time discussing *Oliver Twist* when children worked from morning till night in factories only a few miles away? Children who could be helped.

There was work to be done in the world, and for the first time women were doing it. Emma Goldman, the famous anarchist, was in the thick of every fight for social reform. Isadora Duncan, the American dancer, was creating a sensation, both in her art and in her personal life.

Isadora didn't care in the least about being respectable. *She* wanted to be independent. Margaret looked at her own strait-laced way of life and—like hundreds of other women—envied Isadora.

Margaret's one real comfort was her family. She adored

Margaret Sanger with her first child, Stuart, in 1904.

Stuart, now a sturdy four-year-old. Moreover, she was expecting another baby.

By now the house was nearly finished, and Bill and Margaret were eager to move into it. So they sent for the treasured possessions they had left in storage—their books and rugs and works of art.

It was early February 1908 when the vans drove up and the crates and boxes were unloaded. Margaret and Bill built a roaring fire and kept it going as they unpacked their things and put them away. They worked through the day and well into the night. Both were exhausted long before they were finished.

At last they went to bed, and Margaret dropped off to sleep at once. Within a few minutes, though, the screams of the maid awakened her. "Fire!" she shrieked. "Fire! The house is on fire!"

Margaret snatched Stuart from his crib and dashed to safety. Bill rushed to a neighbor's to call the fire department—their own telephone had not yet been installed. Then the two stood together, holding hands under the frosty sky and watched as the flames destroyed their dream house and all their cherished belongings.

Margaret was close to tears as the house and all its furnishings crumbled to ashes. Yet she felt a strange relief. She felt, she said later, as if a terrible burden had been lifted from her shoulders, as if her very spirit had been set free.

The house was rebuilt very soon. Margaret and Bill moved into it right away. But there was no longer any magic, any joy, to it. It was a house, not a home.

Then the Sanger's second son was born. Grant was as perfect as Stuart had been. When Grant was twenty months old, the little girl that Margaret had longed for was born. They named her Peggy.

Margaret was thrilled to hold an infant in her arms again. But as the children reached the toddling stage, she complained that she was "tired of the tame life of the pretty suburb." To a friend she protested, "I'm getting kitchen-minded."

Quickly, though, Margaret found a remedy. First she turned to reading, then to writing. This meant, of course, that she neglected such household duties as darning and mending. Often the Sanger children went around for days with their clothes pinned together. Finally a neighbor, who admired Margaret for her ambition, took charge of the situation and sewed buttons on jackets and coats.

Bill admired Margaret's ambition, too, and also encouraged her to write. Often he came home to tackle a stack of dishes so that Margaret could finish some article she was working on.

Her subjects were always of political or social interest. Her viewpoint, like that of her father, was left-wing, if not radical.

Bill had always shared Margaret's ideas. He, too, was a Socialist, and it was a source of never-ending pride to Michael Higgins that his son-in-law was a personal friend of the great Socialist leader, Eugene V. Debs.

Bill knew many other radical thinkers, too. Sometimes one would make the trip to Hastings to spend an evening in discussion with the Sangers. At times like that, their living room seemed just like Michael Higgins's workshop, with views expressed that were far more extreme than those heard at the usual Hastings social gathering.

Margaret longed to break away from the small town. Her chance came at last when Bill accepted an important commission in New Jersey. It would keep him busy a full year. During it, he would have to live in New York, since the daily trip to Hastings was too strenuous.

It was a moment when the Sanger family fortunes were at a low ebb. Margaret's help was needed to pay the bills which had piled up. Bill's mother was now living with the couple, and she could be counted on to care for the children while Margaret worked as a nurse.

The house in Hastings was sold, and the Sangers moved into a comfortable, if not fashionable, apartment in New York. Both Margaret and Bill at once plunged into the reform movements popular with their friends.

One night, Margaret was asked to pinch-hit for a speaker at a Socialist meeting. She knew little about labor—the subject planned—so she lectured instead on health and hygiene, discussing the specific problems of women, especially those connected with marriage. She was surprised at the interest of her audience, who asked question after question. She was even more surprised when the editor of *The Call*, the Socialist weekly, suggested she write some articles for the paper, along the lines of her speech.

There were two series of such articles. One was called "What Every Mother Should Know"; the second, "What Every Girl Should Know." Often Margaret wrote her column as she sat by the bed of a sleeping patient. At other times she worked on it after she returned from a nursing stint, sometimes staying up until the early hours to meet her deadline.

In those days before the First World War, most women had their babies at home. Those of the very poor were delivered by midwives, women skilled at assisting other women in childbirth, who made a profession of it. Only if a woman's life was in danger would a doctor be called. He, in turn, might send for a nurse.

Many such nursing jobs fell to Margaret. The telephone

would ring in the middle of the night, and she would be summoned to a dingy tenement.

Margaret was shocked at the misery of the slums. Sometimes eight or ten people lived, crowded together, in a couple of dark, filthy rooms. There were no baths in the buildings, and running water only on every other floor. Toilets were usually outdoors.

No sun, no air, entered such lodgings. Some rooms had no windows at all. Others had only small high ones, which opened onto garbage-filled air shafts.

Time after time the women Margaret cared for admitted they hadn't wanted another baby. "We already have more than we can feed," they would add.

The pinched faces of the wretched children, shoeless, dressed in rags, was proof of that. By the time they were eight or nine years old, they had forgotten how to laugh. They looked like old men and women, their eyes always filled with fear. Many already went out to work in sweatshops. Others worked at home, picking over rags to be made into artificial flowers, or making lampshades.

Sometimes the mothers told Margaret of their poverty. "My husband's a good man, but he only works two or three days a week." Sometimes they talked of hereditary diseases. "Joe's an epileptic!" "There's insanity in the family." The women's stories might be different, but they all added up to the same fact: there were simply too many children in each family.

As Margaret listened, her thoughts often went back to the Christmas Eve, years before, when her youngest brother was born. He was the tenth child, and Annie Higgins could only look at him in despair and whisper, "Oh, God! Oh, my God!"

Just as the women told Margaret the stories of their lives, they invariably asked her one question. "Mrs. Sanger," they said, "how can I keep from having another baby?"

Margaret knew that they had tried one useless method after another to get rid of an unborn child. When home remedies failed, they went to the abortionists in the neighborhood. Often, in the evenings, Margaret saw as many as a hundred women waiting in line for them. Each would pay a few dollars for a quick operation. After five or ten minutes' rest, they would go home.

All too often, infections set in a day or so later. Women at death's door would be rushed to hospitals. Of those lucky enough to return home, many were crippled for life. Those, like Sadie Sachs, who performed abortions on themselves, were even more likely to die.

Margaret was called to nurse Sadie back to health by her husband, Jake. In a choked voice, he poured out her story. She was only twenty-eight, he explained, and the mother of three children. "We love them, Mrs. Sanger," he insisted. "But I don't make enough money to care for *them*. How can we feed another?"

He came home one evening to find Sadie lying unconscious on the floor. The crying children huddled in a corner. Jake called a doctor at once, and then he sent for Margaret. He had put aside a few pennies each week, against a rainy day. Now he drew his savings from the bank to pay Margaret. Sadie, he swore, would never go to a hospital—too many women died in hospitals.

It was July, and New York sweltered in a blistering heat wave. For three weeks, in record-breaking temperatures, Margaret ran up and down stairs, carrying water, bringing ice for Sadie. At last Mrs. Sachs was pronounced out of danger, and Margaret prepared to leave.

But Sadie was depressed, worried about something. It was a day or so before she had the courage to tell Margaret what it was. Then, in a weak little voice she said, "Another baby will finish me, I suppose."

Margaret did her best to comfort Sadie. "It's too early to talk about that, Mrs. Sachs," she told her. But she made up her mind to mention it to the doctor. Later, as he took Sadie's pulse, she said, "Mrs. Sachs is worried about having another baby."

"She should be!" he answered, pressing Sadie's wrist with his finger while he held his gold pocket watch to his ear. "Any more of *this* and she won't need *me!*"

For a moment Sadie was silent. Then she whispered, "But what can I do to prevent getting that way again?"

The doctor let out a hearty laugh. "So, you want to eat your cake and have it, too," he said. "Well, tell Jake to sleep on the roof." He picked up his bag and left. As the door slammed behind him, Sadie burst into tears.

"Oh, Mrs. Sanger," she said between sobs, "you understand, don't you? You're a woman, and you'll tell me, and I'll never tell a soul."

But Margaret couldn't tell her! She knew of certain methods, but surely Sadie knew of those, too. Anyway, it was up to the husband to use them. Margaret knew of nothing women could use to keep from becoming pregnant.

Still, she could hardly admit that to Sadie, pathetic as she was. Instead she said, "I'll come back in a few days. Then I'll tell you."

But Margaret could think of nothing to say, nothing to do, that would offer Sadie hope. Dreading to see her disappointment, Margaret let the days pass while she made excuses to herself. Then, three months later, there was another desperate telephone call from Jacob Sachs. "Please come," he begged.

Margaret knew at once that Sadie had become pregnant

again. This time she had gone to an abortionist. It had cost her five dollars—and would cost her life.

As Margaret walked into Sadie's room, the doctor—the same doctor—looked up from her bedside and shook his head.

Ten minutes later, Sadie Sachs was dead.

Chapter 4

THE GREAT DECISION

THAT NIGHT, Margaret wandered for hours through the narrow streets of the Lower East Side. Men sat on fire escapes, often in their undershirts; women in faded cotton dresses called to one another.

Margaret neither saw nor heard them. She walked as if in a trance, scarcely feeling the heat, while Jacob Sachs's shrill, heartbroken cry echoed in her ears.

It was three in the morning when Margaret reached home. She had walked all the way—from one end of Manhattan to the other—and was exhausted. Yet she could not sleep.

Still clutching her nurse's satchel, she stood at the window and stared at the dark outline of the buildings beyond. Their walls seemed to disappear, and Margaret saw only the misery within them.

She saw the thousands of women in the agony of labor. She saw the infants born to them—sickly, wrapped in newspapers to keep them from the cold. She saw the hungry, neglected children—the ailing, the deformed.

Her sight shifted from the buildings to the streets. Processions of coffins seemed to pass. There were tiny white ones for the babies, black ones for their mothers. On and on they came—on and on! Hot as the night was, a cold chill ran up Margaret's spine.

She shook herself, and her thoughts drifted back to Corning.

Sometimes, as a small child, she had slipped away from home, crossed the river, and climbed the hill to the "good" section of the city. The streets there were broad and clean, shaded by leafy trees. Houses were large and freshly painted. Behind lace curtains, she glimpsed beautiful furniture, thick carpets, fresh flowers in silver bowls.

Outdoors, families relaxed, playing croquet or even tennis, or simply sipping cold drinks as they lounged in swings. Margaret, peering between the iron spikes of the fences, felt a twinge of envy at the starched, beribboned dresses of the little girls. How pleasant it would be to have brand-new clothes instead of hand-me-downs!

It occurred to Margaret that the families on the hill were small. She never saw more than two or three children in each. Where she lived, each family had at least six offspring and sometimes as many as twelve.

How curious that was! Wealthy families, who could care for many children, had only a few, while poor families were constantly burdened with another infant.

Gradually, Margaret saw that that was only part of the

picture. While wealthy people might be able to afford large families and see that each child was well fed, well clothed, even well educated, that was hardly the case among the poor. There, more children merely meant that all were likely to go hungry.

Her father's endless schemes for utopia—for a heaven on earth—now seemed ridiculous. The remedies for the ills of the world proposed by the Socialist Party were just as absurd. What good was it for workers to own the factories if each worker's share was too little to feed his large family? A raise in wages each year meant nothing if there was a new baby each year, too. The few extra dollars would go to care for the infant, while the others struggled along as before. As for shorter working hours, wasn't a woman's health broken more by constant child-bearing than by long hours in a factory?

Margaret thought of all the books her father had treasured, those she herself quoted. Sadie Sachs had read none of them. Yet she had known far more than Margaret. She had understood the simple fact that she and Jake could not support another child.

Margaret still stood at the window, staring at the silent city. As she did, the sun came into view, painting the sky a pale pink. It was a new day—more than that, it was the beginning of a new life for Margaret. She would never again, she swore, nurse a woman like Sadie Sachs back to health and leave her to face the same dilemma again. Instead, she would give such women the information they begged for.

Just then she noticed that she was still clutching her nurse's bag. With a sigh of relief she threw it across the room. She tore off her uniform, and hurled *it* into a corner. As the first rays of the rising sun appeared, she went to her room and crawled into bed. For the first time in months she slept peacefully.

When Margaret awoke, she began to map her plans. If, as she had vowed, she would teach women what they begged to know, she must have that information herself. That, she thought, she would easily get from doctors.

But none was willing to give it to her!

Some doctors simply told Margaret that no "magic formula" existed. Others rudely ordered her to "leave at once." Then Margaret went to druggists. They were at least more friendly. Some even tried to be helpful. But the information they gave her was, at best, useless. Often, it was harmful.

Libraries? Margaret searched them. Even medical texts told her nothing.

Yet *someone* knew the answer. Who? And who would give it to Margaret?

When she asked her friends, most of them threw their hands up in horror. It was all well and good to limit families, they agreed. But Margaret was headed for trouble if she tried to explain how. After all, they warned, there was Anthony Comstock to be reckoned with.

Margaret had plenty of reason to be wary of *that* old man. In one of the pieces she had written for *The Call*, she discussed quite frankly, and in medical terms, a venereal disease. That Sunday she turned to the woman's page to see her literary effort in print. There was the title, "What Every Girl Should Know." But it was at the head of two blank columns! Only a single word, "Nothing!" was printed under it.

Any mention of syphilis, Margaret learned, was considered obscene and therefore banned. The man responsible for this state of affairs was Anthony Comstock, founder and secretary of the New York Society for the Suppression of Vice.

To Comstock, almost anything was sinful, from medical

books to some of the most famous works of art and the greatest
literature. And Comstock's power was almost as broad as his
mind was narrow. Thanks to him, laws were passed in New
York State against "immoral" books and pictures. Thanks also
to Comstock, federal postal laws were strengthened, so that
heavy fines and even long jail terms awaited those who mailed
anything *he*, personally, found offensive.

Margaret bristled at the mere mention of Comstock's name.
But she would never let him stop her! "I will be heard," she
insisted. "If I have to scream from the housetops, I *will* be
heard!"

Bill, too, had decided to be heard—or at least seen. It was
the spring of 1913, and the famous Armory Show had set all
New York talking. For the first time, works of ultramodern
French artists were displayed in America. Included was the
Cubist painting *Nude Descending a Staircase*, which looked
more like squares and boxes than a human figure. Many people
laughed at it, but Bill Sanger saw it for the masterpiece it was.

It made him long to paint, more than ever. He was heartily
sick of designing other people's houses by now. Moreover, the
Sangers now had a tidy little nest egg set aside, mainly from
the sale of their Hastings house. It would get the entire family
across the ocean and keep them in modest comfort for a year
or two.

With all that had to be attended to, they could not sail until
the fall. So Margaret and the children spent the summer months
in the little Cape Cod town of Truro, where Bill joined them
on week-ends.

The small fishing village was hardly known in those days.
The Sangers, with a few of their friends, had it almost to them-

selves. Margaret was grateful for that. Now she had time to romp with little Peggy on the sandy beach, to show Grant how to fish or Stuart how to sail. But when the children were safely tucked in bed at night, she spoke to the others of the subject that was almost always on her mind.

They, too, were concerned at the wretched state of so many millions of women. But few were willing to encourage Margaret in what they thought of as a mad scheme. Not only did they warn her again against Comstock; most of them also told her to wait.

"Wait until women vote," the Suffragettes said. "Then we'll change the laws." "Wait until the Socialists run the government," *they* said. "Then poverty will disappear." Only the anarchists were willing to join Margaret.

"Big Bill" Haywood, the organizer for the Industrial Workers of the World, was especially sympathetic. The IWW was the most radical of all labor organizations, and "Big Bill" had shown unbelievable courage in fighting against oppression.

He had risked his life to lead strikes in the copper mines of Utah and the lumber camps of the Pacific Northwest. He had often been attacked and injured. Some of his friends had been killed; he himself had lost an eye.

Unlike all the others, he urged her not to lose a minute. He was especially enthusiastic about the Sangers' plans to go to Paris. "The French have been limiting their families for a hundred years," he told her. "That's where you'll get your information. Right at the source. Right from the women themselves."

Hadn't Emma Goldman done just that, ten years earlier, when she'd been a delegate to the very first conference on poverty and population? That had been in Paris, of course. Emma, who had been a nurse like Margaret, had learned some of the methods the French women used. But she had been there such a short time! What luck that Bill and Margaret were planning a long stay!

On a blustery day in October 1913 Margaret and Bill, with the three children, sailed from Boston. They stopped briefly in Glasgow, Scotland, where Margaret wrote several articles for *The Call.* They spent a night or so in London. Then they crossed the Channel to the French capital.

In almost no time the whole family felt at home in Paris. They rented an apartment overlooking the Luxembourg Gardens, a few minutes' walk from the studio Bill took at Montparnasse. He painted happily all day, while the children struggled with French verbs in the local *école maternelle,* and Margaret continued her quest.

She called on the dozens of distinguished French men and women to whom she had introductions. When she explained her mission, all were eager to help her.

They took her to meet the average middle-class woman in her home; to meet the wives of workers at union meetings, or in small cafés. She spoke to servants, to laundresses, to shop girls. She questioned each of them about her family. "How is it you have only one child?" Or two. Or three. "Yet you've been married ten years?"

The women, being French, shrugged their shoulders. "But Madame! My Pierre and I didn't want more than that!"

"But where did you learn how to prevent pregnancies?"

"Why, from *Maman!*" the women answered.

"And where did *she* learn?" Margaret went on.

Grant, Peggy, and Stuart Sanger in Paris, 1913.

"Why, from *Grand-maman*!"

When Margaret asked the women what they had learned from Maman or Grand-maman, they told her gladly. Most were surprised that Margaret was even interested. Didn't American women know such things already?

Margaret rushed around, making careful notes, writing out instructions, buying the products French women used. In a few months she was almost frantic to leave Paris. Her real work, giving American women the information she had gathered, lay ahead. Each day she lingered in France, lives were lost.

It had been a fruitful trip for Margaret. For Bill, it was one of ups and downs. He enjoyed his own work so much that he willingly put up with his wife's changing moods for a while. He soothed her when she was outraged; he cheered her when everything seemed hopeless. And he made do with a thoroughly disorganized household.

Meals were often late; sometimes, too, Margaret was too busy to order food for dinner. Fortunately for the children, the little maid took care of all their needs. As for Bill, he munched a bit of bread or went to a restaurant. At other times the place was so full of people that the din was deafening. Bill, who had nothing in common with Margaret's new friends, felt left out.

The first weeks in Paris were often difficult for Bill; the last few were impossible. Living with Margaret was like living with a volcano—one that might erupt at any moment.

At last Bill and Margaret faced the situation squarely. He was content with his work, his new way of life. Furthermore, success was just beginning to come his way. To leave now would destroy his career.

Under the circumstances, the Sangers decided to part. Bill would stay in Paris and paint. Margaret would return to New

York. It was to be, they told each other, only a temporary arrangement.

So, on New Year's Day, 1914, Margaret, with the three Sanger children, sailed for home.

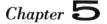

Chapter 5

THE WOMAN REBEL

MARGARET SPENT the long voyage home making plans. Before she was halfway across the Atlantic, she resolved to publish a magazine "for the advancement of women's freedom." Before she landed, she had decided on a name for it: *The Woman Rebel.*

Her first move, though, when she reached New York, was to find an apartment which would be home for herself and the children, as well as her office. She stumbled on just the thing she had in mind, at the upper end of Manhattan Island. She could work in the dining room there, using the table as her desk.

Margaret's next job was to raise some money. There would be no salaries to be paid; Margaret planned to do most of the work herself. Still, money was needed to print and mail the eight-page monthly magazine.

Margaret had almost none herself. Bill had shared what he had with her, but that would go for food and rent. So Margaret turned to her friends.

Sure enough, money began to trickle in—five dollars here, ten there. Emma Goldman went to work and raised much more. But the total wasn't nearly enough to pay the bills already piled on Margaret's desk. She went blithely ahead, though, steadily adding to them. "They'll get paid somehow," she assured her creditors.

But a magazine without readers was as useless as a penniless publisher. Margaret, scouting around for readers, sent notices about *The Woman Rebel* to five or six radical papers that appeared—rather irregularly—in those days. Then she had leaflets printed.

They urged everyone who wanted to do away with the "slavery of women" to read the new magazine. Margaret made it plain, too, that women were slaves because of "motherhood, wages, bourgeois morality, customs, laws, and superstitions." Satisfied that her appeal would both attract attention and bring in subscribers, Margaret tucked a big bundle of the handbills under her arm every evening. Then she went around to union meetings and handed them out.

Just as she had expected, subscriptions to *The Woman Rebel* began arriving in the mail. Then her friends began turning up on her doorstep, usually in the evening after work. What could they do to help?

Margaret set them to work at whatever needed doing. They typed letters and addressed envelopes and stamped them. Those who had literary skills wrote articles.

After their tasks were finished, her friends often stayed on to talk. Infected by Margaret's enthusiasm, they were almost as ardent as she about her "cause." But one night someone complained that it had no name. They were, after all, starting a new movement. What was it to be called?

"Conscious generation?"

That wasn't very catchy. Neither was "voluntary parenthood."

"Birth-rate control?" Everyone shook his head.

"Why not drop the 'rate,' then?" Margaret asked. "Call it birth control." Triumphantly she repeated, "Birth control." And "birth control" became the name of the new movement.

In the next days and weeks, work went ahead on *The Woman Rebel*. At last the first issue was ready. Proudly, Margaret mailed the magazine, dated "March, 1914," to her handful of subscribers.

They opened it to find that Margaret Higgins Sanger was declaring her independence—and that of every other woman. She intended to flaunt the laws of Comstock—she considered him the scourge of the earth—and she made matters more plain by printing the laws themselves.

Among other things, the laws stated that information about limiting families was obscene, and Margaret answered with the statement that "a woman's body belongs to herself alone!"

Emma Goldman, in that first issue, said almost the same thing, although in different words. Women were not machines, she declared. So why should they bear children unless they wanted to?

The little paper was designed to shock, and it did. Not content with her comments on the rights of women and her stand on birth control, Margaret brought in every radical idea she could think of.

THE WOMAN REBEL

NO GODS NO MASTERS

VOL I.   MARCH 1914   NO. 1.

THE AIM

This paper will not be the champion of any "ism."

All rebel women are invited to contribute to its columns.

The majority of papers usually adjust themselves to the ideas of their readers but the WOMAN REBEL will obstinately refuse to be adjusted.

The aim of this paper will be to stimulate working women to think for themselves and to build up a conscious fighting character.

An early feature will be a series of articles written by the editor for girls from fourteen to eighteen years of age. In this present chaos of sex atmosphere it is difficult for the girl of this uncertain age to know just what to do or really what constitutes clean living without prudishness. All this slushy talk about white slavery, the man painted and described as a hideous vulture pouncing down upon the young, pure and innocent girl, drugging her through the medium of grape juice and lemonade and then dragging her off to his foul den for other men equally as vicious to feed and fatten on her enforced slavery — surely this picture is enough to sicken and disgust every thinking woman and man, who has lived even a few years past the adolescent age. Could any more repulsive and foul conception of sex be given to adolescent girls as a preparation for life than this picture that is being perpetuated by the stupidly ignorant in the name of "sex education"?

If it were possible to get the truth from girls who work in prostitution to-day, I believe most of them would tell you that the first sex experience was with a sweetheart or through the desire for a sweetheart or something impelling within themeselves, the nature of which they knew not, neither could they control. Society does not forgive this act when it is based upon the natural impulses and feelings of a young girl. It prefers the other story of the grape juice procurer which makes it easy to shift the blame from its own shoulders, to cast the stone and to evade the unpleasant facts that it alone is responsible for. It sheds sympathetic tears over white slavery, holds the often mythical procurer up as a target, while in reality it is supported by the misery it engenders.

If, as reported, there are approximately 35,000 women working as prostitutes in New York City alone, is it not sane to conclude that some force, some living, powerful, social force is at play to compel these women to work at a trade which involves police persecution, social ostracism and the constant danger of exposure to venereal diseases. From my own knowledge of adolescent girls and from sincere expressions of women working as prostitutes inspired by mutual understanding and confidence I claim that the first sexual act of these so-called wayward girls is partly given, partly desired yet reluctantly so because of the fear of the consequences together with the dread of lost respect of the man. These fears interfere with mutuality of expression —the man becomes conscious of the responsibility of the act and often refuses to see her again, sometimes leaving the town and usually denouncing her as having been with "other fel-

lows." His sole aim is to throw off responsibility. The same uncertainty in these emotions is experienced by girls in marriage in as great a proportion as in the unmarried. After the first experience the life of a girl varies. All these girls do not necessarily go into prostitution. They have had an experience which has not "ruined" them, but rather given them a larger vision of life, stronger feelings and a broader understanding of human nature. The adolescent girl does not understand herself. She is full of contradictions, whims, emotions. For her emotional nature longs for caresses, to touch, to kiss. She is often as well satisfied to hold hands or to go arm in arm with a girl as in the companionship of a boy.

It is these and kindred facts upon which the WOMAN REBEL will dwell from time to time and from which it is hoped the young girl will derive some knowledge of her nature, and conduct her life upon such knowledge.

It will also be the aim of the WOMAN REBEL to advocate the prevention of conception and to impart such knowledge in the columns of this paper.

Other subjects, including the slavery through motherhood; through things, the home, public opinion and so forth, will be dealt with.

It is also the aim of this paper to circulate among those women who work in prostitution; to voice their wrongs; to expose the police persecution which hovers over them and to give free expression to their thoughts, hopes and opinions.

And at all times the WOMAN REBEL will strenuously advocate economic emancipation.

THE NEW FEMINISTS

That apologetic tone of the new American feminists which plainly says "Really, Madam Public Opinion, we are all quite harmless and perfectly respectable" was the keynote of the first and second mass meetings held at Cooper Union on the 17th and 20th of February last.

The ideas advanced were very old and time-worn even to the ordinary church-going woman who reads the magazines and comes in contact with current thought. The "right to work," the "right to ignore fashions," the "right to keep her own name," the "right to organize," the "right of the mother to work"; all these so-called rights fail to arouse enthusiasm because to-day they are all recognized by society and there exist neither laws nor strong opposition to any of them.

It is evident they represent a middle class woman's movement; an echo, but a very weak echo, of the English constitutional suffragists. Consideration of the working woman's freedom was ignored. The problems which affect the

—New York Public Library

The first issue of *The Woman Rebel,* March 1914.

She printed the Preamble to the Constitution—of the Industrial Workers of the World! A poem by an anarchist in praise of bombing "the enemies of the people" was prominently featured in *The Woman Rebel.*

But no matter what else Margaret printed, she always came back to the subject of women and their rights. If they wanted to be lazy—fine! If they wanted to be mothers, that was fine, too, and it shouldn't matter in the least whether or not they were married.

On the other hand, there was no reason in the world why a woman should be a mother if she didn't want children. Women were to be free, FREE, FREE! They had one duty, and one alone. That was "to look the world in the face with a go-to-hell look in the eyes; to have an idea; to speak and act in defiance of convention."

Margaret expected to stir up a storm with such comments. It wasn't long in coming. Newspapers like the Pittsburgh *Sun* attacked her, writing of *The Woman Rebel,* "The thing is nauseating." Even Max Eastman, whose own views were so extreme that he served as editor of the Communist paper *The Masses,* thought Margaret's paper an example of "very conscious extremism and rebellion for its own sake."

Many of the women Margaret hoped would support her agreed with Eastman and began to edge away. "This time," they told one another, "Margaret Sanger has gone too far."

Too far?

Yes, Margaret admitted, if you thought "emancipation" meant keeping your maiden name after marriage, as the "Lucy Stoners" did. Or thought it "revolutionary" to refuse to wear a wedding ring.

Too far? Not far enough for the women who were already

writing Margaret, telling her the pathetic stories of their lives and begging for contraceptive techniques.

Margaret was sitting at her desk, opening a batch of such letters one morning just a month after *The Woman Rebel* first appeared, when an official-looking envelope from the New York Post Office caught her eye. She tore it open and read the enclosed letter. The March issue of *The Woman Rebel,* the postmaster informed her, had been found "unmailable under the provisions of Section 211 of the Criminal Code . . ."

But it was not against the law to speak out in favor of birth control! It was only illegal to tell women the means and methods of it. Margaret hadn't done that—not yet!

She pushed aside the pile of unanswered letters, the other pile of unpaid bills, and dashed off a note to the postmaster. Just which articles in *The Woman Rebel* had he objected to? she asked. A few days later the postmaster wrote back. *The Woman Rebel,* he said again, was unmailable. He told Margaret nothing more.

Unmailable! Then copies had been seized. But to judge from the letters coming in, others had been delivered. Margaret, puzzled, hurried to the post office to make a few inquiries.

There she learned that half the mailing list—copies sent to those with names beginning with letters from A to M—had, indeed, been seized and burned. The rest had been delivered, like ordinary mail, without trouble.

Margaret quickly thought of a way to outwit the postmaster. There were still plenty of copies of that first issue of *The Woman Rebel* filling the closets of her apartment. She called the friends who had helped earlier with the magazine.

That evening they sat around Margaret's dining-room table and addressed a second batch of magazines. Then, when it was very dark, they stole out into the night. Each of them carried about twenty copies of *The Woman Rebel*.

The group quickly split up, going in all directions. Some went uptown, some down. Some headed toward the Hudson, others toward the East River. As they tramped the streets, they dropped copies of *The Woman Rebel*—one by one—in postal chutes.

It was dawn before many of them reached their homes. But Margaret's scheme worked. Even the eagle-eyed postal inspectors never noticed that the magazine had been mailed, and this time, copies of it went to subscribers without a hitch.

From that moment Margaret knew she would have a fight on her hands. She had deliberately broken the law, well aware that for just this one violation she could be fined one thousand dollars and sent to jail for five years. Moreover, she intended to do it again—and again—and again.

Margaret had no desire to become a martyr. Yet she would not—*could* not—give up the magazine. Too many women needed her help. She refused to let them down.

For the next eight months Margaret spent every spare moment on the work she had cut out for herself. There was so little time left! Comstock and the post office, along with every Mrs. Grundy in America, were closing in on her. Before they did, she must get her message across.

Each month she published another issue of *The Woman Rebel*. Three of these were banned from the mails, too. But Margaret simply sent out the copies the way she had before— late at night, one by one, from mail chutes throughout New York.

Margaret's day was full enough, taken up with caring for her own family, as well as publishing *The Woman Rebel*. Yet the letters that poured in, begging for definite advice on contraception, convinced her that her work had hardly begun.

In eight months Margaret received more than ten thousand such letters, far too many for her to answer individually. Instead, she wrote a small pamphlet, *Family Limitation*, giving her readers all the information she had promised them. It was couched in clear and simple terms, with instructions any woman could follow.

Margaret knew that most printers would turn down her manuscript, so she took it to one whose ideas were almost as radical as her own. He read the first few pages and turned a ghostly white. "I can't print that, Margaret. That's a Sing Sing job," he said, naming the state prison.

She took her manuscript to a second printer, then a third. Always the answer was the same. "I wouldn't dare!" By the end of the week Margaret had heard it twenty times.

At last she thought of Bill Shatoff, an anarchist as spunky as she was. Shatoff wasn't a printer, but a linotype operator on a foreign-language newspaper. Even so, Margaret went to see him, and Shatoff agreed to do the job.

Each night for weeks, after hours, he stole into the printing shop where he worked during the day. There, alone, he set the type, inked the presses, and pulled the sheets.

Margaret had ordered 100,000 copies of *Family Limitation*. As they were delivered, she and her friends addressed them, made them up into small, carefully wrapped packages, and shipped them to sympathizers from coast to coast. They would distribute them when the time was ripe.

One warm afternoon there was a knock at the door of Margaret's apartment. She opened the door to find two men standing outside. "Are you Mrs. Margaret Sanger?" they asked politely.

Margaret admitted that she was.

"The editor and publisher of *The Woman Rebel?*"

Margaret admitted that, too. Then the men handed her a thick document.

As Margaret read it, she trembled. It was difficult to understand, written in complicated legal language which makes sense only to lawyers. Yet Margaret realized that she had been indicted on nine different criminal charges, all in connection with *The Woman Rebel.* She must appear in court later that month, when a trial date would be set. If, at the trial, she was convicted on all counts, she faced *forty-five years* in prison!

Still shaking, Margaret invited the men in and began to explain her fight for birth control. She told them of the misery of mothers, of the suffering of children, of her hope to help them. For two hours she talked while they listened attentively. When they left, they, too, seemed convinced of the need to limit families.

Before her hearing, Margaret was unconcerned. Surely the judge was a reasonable man—like the two federal agents—who would see that justice was on her side and dismiss the charges. But when Margaret appeared before him, he ordered her tried within six weeks.

Then Margaret's friends came flocking around, offering advice. Almost everyone knew a lawyer who could "get her off" on a technicality. Others urged her to plead guilty and promise to obey the law from then on. If she did, sentence might be suspended.

Margaret refused to listen. What was she guilty of? The law said she printed "obscene material." Was it "obscene" to save women's lives. No, birth control was not "obscene." Margaret was not guilty. It was the law that was wrong.

For the next six weeks Margaret lived in an eerie world. Once, as a child, she was walking across a railroad trestle when a train came along. In the nick of time she slipped down between two ties, hanging desperately to them while her feet dangled way above the ground. There she stayed until the train passed and she was rescued.

Now she seemed to walk along that same trestle, while that same train hurtled toward her. But she could not even *try* to save herself.

In her strange dream world, Margaret kept on walking. In real life she went on with her work. Two more issues of *The Woman Rebel* were finished and sent out. Elaborate plans were made to distribute *Family Limitation*. Above all, arrangements were made for the care of Stuart, Grant, and Peggy.

Margaret had not yet hired a lawyer when her case was called. She only learned the day and hour of the hearing from the district attorney. Therefore, in court, she asked for a month's postponement to prepare her defense. But now the judge was grim. Banging his gavel, he ordered the trial to begin that afternoon.

Margaret spent the lunch recess tracking down a lawyer. He, too, asked for a delay. It was granted, but only until the next morning.

Sick at heart, Margaret went home, pondering what to do. Plead guilty, as even the lawyer suggested? If she did, she would be silenced forever. But if she went to jail, she would be silenced, too:

"I will be heard!" she had sworn. "If I have to scream from the housetops, I *will* be heard." There was only one way.

For the moment Margaret needed complete quiet, complete solitude. She packed a suitcase and checked in at a small hotel.

There she wrote a note to the judge, explaining her actions. She wrote to Bill Sanger, who was back in New York, asking him to care for the children.

She called a taxi then, and went to Grand Central Station. There she took the midnight train to Canada.

Chapter **6**

EXILE

THE NEXT MORNING Margaret stepped off the train in Montreal. She had left behind all that was dear to her— her children, her home, her friends. Yet she was still not beyond the reach of the American courts. Since she had been charged with a felony, she could be arrested in Canada and brought back to New York, handcuffed to a bailiff.

It was a dismal thought, but Margaret was cheered to spy friends waiting for her on the platform. They took her home with them, then set about arranging for her to get to England.

It took all their influence, as well as one stroke of luck after

another, to do so. It was October 1914 and the terrible First
World War was raging, with Britain deeply engaged in fighting.
The country was hardly likely to welcome a fugitive from
American justice who had neither a passport nor any identifica-
tion papers.

Still, Margaret managed to book passage aboard the Canadian
ship R.M.S. *Virginian*, crossing the Atlantic with a cargo of
munitions. When it sailed, a few weeks later, a pretty, young
red-headed woman who called herself "Bertha Watson" was
on board.

Margaret, or "Bertha Watson," soon made friends with other
passengers, who promised to help her. When they reached
Liverpool, one persuaded the British authorities to let Bertha
land, while another got in touch with officials at the American
Embassy in London and insisted that they give her a passport.

As usual, Margaret had plenty of letters of introduction in
her handbag. Most of them had been given to her by her
Canadian friends. They were written to people both in England
and on the Continent. Thanks to them, she would have no
trouble getting on with her business.

Meanwhile, when the *Virginian* was three days at sea, Margaret attended to some unfinished business at home. From the
ship, she sent telegrams to four faithful allies. She asked each
to call together the group of friends who knew Margaret's secret
plan and put it into action.

They did so at once. They gathered up the copies of *Family
Limitation* which had been hidden in warehouses, closets, and
attics all across the country. Then they mailed them, in small
bundles and batches, a few here, a few there, just as they had
mailed *The Woman Rebel*.

Soon after Margaret reached London, she looked up the

leaders of the growing British birth-control movement. Even those to whom she had no introduction welcomed her. Like the others, they had heard of her work. Many even had copies of *The Woman Rebel* on their desks.

Kind as all were to Margaret, she was unbearably lonely through the fall and winter. London was bitterly cold and damp, as it usually was in the winter. Margaret's own small room, on an upper floor of an inexpensive hotel, seemed no warmer than the streets outside.

During the days Margaret worked at the British Museum, a block or so away. That, at least, was comfortably heated. But in the evenings she huddled in her drab quarters, wrapping herself in all her sweaters and coats against the chill. Once or twice a week she gave herself a special treat by renting another room for a few hours—one with a grate in which she could build a a fire and "thaw out."

Margaret's research, in the Reading Room of the British Museum, now took a new direction. In America she had first looked for some book, some medical text, that would explain the ways and techniques of contraception. Later she had studied statistics on population.

But now she was interested in the *history* of the whole movement—the stories of those who, long before her time, had seen the need for some way of controlling population, of limiting the size of families. As early as 1798, Thomas Malthus wrote a book pointing out that there would soon be far too many people in the world for the amount of food that could be produced. There would be frightful starvation if something was not done. Malthus, therefore, suggested that men and women marry late in life, limiting the years during which they could have children.

Margaret Sanger in England, 1914.

After Malthus came a host of others—philosophers, economists, and even philanthropists. Margaret read them all.

She had a special reason for doing so. She would cite these great thinkers when she went back to New York to go on trial. They would be her witnesses for the defense.

News from New York that December drove Margaret on and on in her task. When she opened a letter from Bill, she was stunned to learn that he had been arrested.

A man knocked at his door, Bill explained, and begged him for a copy of *Family Limitation*. At first Bill refused. But the man gave him such a sad story about his sick wife and starving children that Bill's heart melted. When the man insisted that he was a friend of Margaret's—in fact, that she had sent him for the pamphlet—Bill gave him a copy.

The next day there was another knock at Bill's door. This time when he opened it, he found a distinguished-looking six-footer. With the utmost courtesy the caller introduced himself: "I am Mr. Comstock."

At that moment Bill's visitor of the day before appeared. Then he called himself "Mr. Heller." Now he admitted that he was Charles Bamburger, an agent for the New York Society for the Suppression of Vice. Furthermore, he had a warrant for the arrest of Sanger, and so the two men led Bill off toward the police station.

They stopped for lunch first, and then spent almost the whole afternoon arguing with Bill. He should plead guilty to the charge against him—distributing obscene literature—they insisted. In addition, he should testify against Margaret.

Indignantly, Bill refused and was finally dragged off to jail. By then it was too late for him to reach a lawyer or to raise the five hundred dollars demanded as bail. He spent thirty-six hours behind bars. Then he was released to stand trial later.

Bill's trial, like Margaret's own, hung over her head. She worked feverishly, gathering as much data as possible, both for her own defense and for Bill's. But a chance remark of the great psychologist Havelock Ellis led her back to the study of statistics.

Ellis was one of Margaret's first friends in London. Long before she met him, she had read everything he had written, difficult though his books were. She hesitated to call on such an important man. When she did, she found him so modest that she felt at ease at once.

Ellis, in turn, was charmed by Margaret's enthusiasm. The woman positively sparkled! From that day until Ellis died, their friendship deepened, and Margaret saw him whenever possible.

At tea, at Ellis's apartment one afternoon, he had spoken of the work being done in Holland in the field of birth control. They were more advanced, more free in their approach, than in any other country. Still, Ellis admitted, there were certain things he himself could not understand . . .

The next day Margaret was at her usual seat in the Reading Room, a stack of books on the great round table in front of her. They were filled with columns of figures, as dull as could be. But as Margaret checked them, she discovered something both curious and fascinating. The birth rate was lower in Holland than any other country in Europe. Yet at the same time, the population was increasing the most rapidly.

Why? It didn't make sense!

It never would, Margaret knew, until she investigated the matter personally. She would go as soon as possible.

She was more than glad to leave London, that January of 1915. Her Christmas had been the gloomiest she could remember. Margaret longed to see her children, to watch their sparkling eyes as they glimpsed the glittering Christmas tree, to see their faces light with joy as they opened their gifts.

There had been scrawled notes—ever so precious to a mother —from all. There had been flowers from ever-thoughtful Bill. And Christmas Eve had been spent with cherished new friends. Still, there was a gnawing emptiness that nothing could ease.

Margaret left it all behind when she crossed the North Sea to Holland.

Her first stop was The Hague, and her first visit to Dr. Johannes Rutgers. The two sat in a café near the palace, over-looking a lake on which swans floated gracefully. There Dr. Rutgers told Margaret of the clinics—fifty-four of them—which had been set up in the small nation.

At each, women could obtain contraceptive supplies. Far more important, the staff at each clinic kept in touch with the women of the neighborhood, as a matter of course. They noted every birth in the district and every death of an infant. When such a tragedy occurred, a nurse was sent to learn why and to help the mother so that her next child might live.

The result, Dr. Rutgers told Margaret in his thick accent, was that children were brought into the world—or at least the world of the Dutch—only when the parents both wanted them and were able to care for them.

At once Margaret saw the answer to the question that had brought her to Holland: why was the population increasing when birth control was being widely practiced?

It was simple. Holland had a lower birth rate than the surrounding countries, but it had a lower *death* rate, too. Fewer children were born but more survived, and those who did survive were bigger and stronger than their parents and grandparents had been.

Margaret listened with rapt attention, then bombarded Dr. Rutgers with questions. What was the average income of these families? How were the fathers employed? Did the mothers work? What were their living conditions? How were they housed?

Dr. Rutgers shook his head. He didn't know, he said. The clinics had neither the time nor the staffs to gather such information.

Margaret was dismayed. So much could be learned if only case histories were carefully kept! She was already turning over in her own mind just such a project as Dr. Rutgers described, but one that would contribute to future knowledge through the very opportunity the Dutch had overlooked.

The idea of clinics—and the hope of establishing them in America—became more and more important to Margaret, traveling through Europe the rest of the winter and spring, settling down in England again for the summer. It was still a far-off dream, of course. Even now, she dared not use her own name with strangers and was always called Bertha Watson. It could be months more, or even years, before she might set foot on American soil again.

But how she longed to! So much time had passed since she had seen her children. She heard from them often enough, as well as from her sister, Nan, who helped Bill care for them. Bill, too, wrote regularly. Always, he and Nan told her the children were healthy and happy, then added the special comments that delighted her. Peggy was learning arithmetic—and actually liked it! Grant's tadpole had sprouted legs; Stuart spent most of his time playing baseball.

The letters and the news cheered Margaret. Yet, at the back of her mind there was the constant fear that something was wrong. It was Peggy she worried about. For no reason at all, she foresaw some terrible disaster. Coupled with that, in her subconscious mind, was the number six.

Margaret did her best to brush away the fear. It was nonsense, she told herself. Peggy was well and happy. The number six? Why, the sixpence she paid for her afternoon tea or the price of the book she bought at the second-hand stall.

But the fear stayed with her, all through the spring and summer. Except for that, the time passed pleasantly enough. Margaret went often to the countryside, where she visited her new friends. She was overjoyed when one of them found a small cottage for Margaret, near her own home.

From there, Margaret made several trips to London to speak to groups of women about birth control. For the first time since she left New York, she appeared in public under her own name. She was Margaret Sanger again, not anonymous little Bertha Watson. That in itself raised her spirits. Along with them, her hopes soared.

Then in September came shattering news. Bill had been brought to trial, found guilty, and sentenced to thirty days in jail.

He had readily admitted he had given out a copy of *Family Limitation*. Yes, he was forbidden to do so by law. Therefore he had broken the law. But the law only prohibited distributing obscene literature. *Family Limitation* was not obscene. Therefore he had *not* broken the law.

The court had been impatient to begin with. Now the black-robed dignitary was furious. Was Bill guilty or not?

"Not guilty."

"Yet you admit giving a copy of *Family Limitation* to this gentleman?" he nodded at Mr. Bamburger.

"Oh, yes."

"Then you plead guilty."

Again, Bill tried to explain: No, he was pleading not guilty.

The judge banged his gavel, ordering Bill to be quiet. Then he barked out his sentence.

Nothing could silence Bill now. He jumped to his feet and shouted, "I want to say to the court that I would rather be in jail with my self-respect than in your place without it!"

At that, the crowd in the courtroom burst into cheers. Again the judge banged for order. No one paid any attention. At last the judge ordered the police to clear the room.

It took them more than ten minutes to do so, as Bill, in a letter to Margaret, reported with just a touch of pride.

Chapter *7*

RETURN

BILL'S LETTER was delivered to Margaret at her little cottage in the country. She read it sitting in the shade of an ancient oak that stood near the door. She read it a second time, then let it flutter to the ground. What was she to do?

Almost a year had passed since she sat in that bleak hotel room just off Times Square, asking herself the same question. What was she to do?

How could she stay on in England, when Bill had been sent to jail? *He* had not written the pamphlet he had given to "Mr. Heller." *He* had not published *The Woman Rebel*. Yet he was behind bars while she sat in the sun in an English garden. She must—she really *must*—go back.

69

But what good would it do if she *did* return? None, Margaret decided. What harm? If she, too, went to jail, a great deal. She owed much to Bill, but she also owed much to the women of America.

She wavered back and forth, trying to make up her mind. Then she gave up. It was impossible to decide.

Finally, though, Margaret found a solution. She would go back to New York. But she wouldn't stay there.

After a few weeks, during which she would find out exactly what was happening, she would leave. She would take the children with her. This time, they would go to France.

So Margaret went house-hunting in Versailles, the village near Paris which had been the home of kings and queens and would now be host to the Sanger family. She found a small place with a garden which would do nicely, signed the lease, and went on to the port city of Bordeaux. From there she sailed for New York.

She slipped back into the country unnoticed, thrilled to be on native soil once more. There was no one to greet her, for even her family had had to be kept in the dark about her venture.

The moment of stepping ashore was so precious to Margaret that she prolonged it by waving away a waiting taxi and walking toward home. Within half an hour, she knew she had come back to a changed land.

She was passing a newsstand, on which the latest issue of *The Pictorial Review*, a popular magazine for women, was displayed. Margaret glanced at it, then turned, amazed, to look again. On the cover was the announcement of the major article in that issue. The title of it was "What Shall We Do About Birth Control?"

Birth control—the words out in the open? And on the cover of a magazine that went into a million homes? Margaret stared in wonder. Could it have been only a year ago that she was charged, like a common criminal, for bringing up the subject in her unprofessional little eight-page paper?

The few letters reaching Margaret during that war year had given her no inkling of this new attitude. She had known, of course, that a national league had been formed to work toward the repeal of the laws against birth control. Now she learned that two outstanding doctors were urging that the matter be carefully studied.

One year! Such a short time for so much progress. Margaret knew that a large part of it was due to sympathy for Bill and public indignation at the shameful way he had been tricked by Anthony Comstock. Much was due, too, to the tireless efforts of the National Birth Control League.

In this new climate Margaret chanced a letter to the judge who would have presided at her trial a year earlier. She sent a similar letter to the prosecuting attorney. Was she, she inquired politely, still to be brought to trial? An answer came from Judge Hazel at once. She was, indeed.

Margaret set out immediately to seek help from the newly formed National Birth Control League, from the newly awakened doctors. She went to them with the highest hopes. For that reason, she was all the more shocked at their refusals to come to her aid. "Why?" Margaret asked. "Why?" Didn't they believe in birth control?

Oh, yes, they assured Margaret. They believed in birth control. But they didn't think Margaret had helped the cause by breaking the law. There were better ways—much better ways —to achieve their aims. So they were very sorry they could do nothing for her.

Margaret was thoroughly depressed after she spoke to them. To make matters worse, Peggy had come down with a cold which hung on for days. Now it turned to pneumonia. As a nurse, Margaret knew how serious the illness was. In those days there were no wonder drugs with which to cure pneumonia.

She sat at the bedside of the little girl, watching her constantly. She sponged her fevered little forehead; she coaxed her to take a spoonful of broth, a sip of water. But Peggy grew steadily worse. Then, on the morning of November 6—the number that had haunted Margaret for months—Peggy died.

Margaret was grief-stricken. To the end of her life, both she and Bill mourned the little girl. But she found some consolation in the thousands of messages of sympathy that came to her from women throughout America. Most knew Margaret Sanger only through her work—through *The Woman Rebel* and *Family Limitation*. They, especially, had been outraged at the harsh punishment meted out to Bill. Now many of them, in spite of crushing poverty, enclosed a few dollars in their letters to Margaret, to be used in her own defense.

Because of Peggy's death, Margaret's trial was postponed for a few weeks. Before it was called, Margaret's friends persuaded her to consult Samuel Untermeyer, a prominent New York lawyer. He received her cordially and listened to her story. Then Untermeyer, by telephone, summoned the prosecuting attorney to his office.

The man Margaret was to face in court arrived a short while later with a thick folder—the file on Margaret's case—under his arm. Untermeyer spoke sternly to the young lawyer. "What are you trying to do?" he asked him. "Persecute this frail little woman . . ." he nodded at Margaret who sat with her hands folded in her lap, a demure expression on her face ". . . the mother of a family?"

The prosecutor looked a trifle sheepish. "We don't want to persecute her," he told Untermeyer. "We don't even want to *prosecute* her. We just want her to promise to obey the law."

"Oh, is that all?" Untermeyer asked. "Well, of course, she'll promise. Now you just drop the case."

When the prosecutor left, taking his thick file with him, Untermeyer beamed at Margaret from behind the vase of red roses on his desk. "Well," he said. "We've fixed that one up. All you have to do is write me a letter and say you won't break the law again."

Margaret, still sitting with her hands folded in her lap, spoke quietly. "But I couldn't promise that, Mr. Untermeyer."

The distinguished old man stared at Margaret, unable to believe his ears. "What?"

"I couldn't promise that, Mr. Untermeyer. I have done nothing obscene, and I refuse to admit that I have." Margaret pulled on her gloves.

For a few minutes Untermeyer pleaded with her. "We *must* keep you from going to jail," he insisted.

Margaret stood and faced her attorney across his desk. "I'm not concerned with going to jail," she informed him. Then she turned and left.

When other lawyers, including even the famous Clarence Darrow, offered to defend Margaret free of charge, she refused their help. "I'm not concerned with going to jail," she repeated. She was certain that no lawyer—a man—could understand her position and that of other women. It was really so simple, though. She was right and the law was wrong.

Why confuse the issue with legal arguments—with "wherefores" and "howsoevers" and "in the instance of the firsts" when you could test the law itself.

That was what Margaret would do. She needed no lawyer for that. She would defend herself.

She called the office of the district attorney and asked that the case be tried immediately. He named a date for it, near the end of November. When that time came, though, he postponed it until January 18. Then he postponed it again, until January 24, 1916.

Long before that day arrived, most of America was taking an interest in the fate of Margaret Sanger. She had many friends among newspaper reporters. They saw to it that her name was mentioned and her cause defended as often as possible.

The idea occurred to one of her newspaper friends to send a photo of Margaret, with Grant and Stuart beside her, to the press. It was published coast to coast and caused a commotion. So *that* was Margaret Sanger, the woman everyone was talking about! But she was a "frail little woman, the mother of a family," as Untermeyer had said.

The public, used to the usual sharp-faced masculine types who fought for women's rights, could hardly believe that someone so feminine, so pretty, would be involved, too. That picture, as the reporter had known, swayed public opinion to Margaret's cause far more than any statement from her could ever have done.

There was support for Margaret from England, too. The friends she had made there during the year she had been away now rallied to her. As a result, a letter from ten outstanding English men and women was laid on the desk of President Woodrow Wilson one morning. It asked that the charges against Margaret be dropped. Since both H. G. Wells and Arnold Bennett, two of the greatest English writers then living, had signed the letter, newspapers found the story worthy of their front pages.

Soon, prominent Americans, too, began to speak out on Margaret's behalf. A group of women, all leaders of New York

Margaret Sanger with Grant and Stuart. This photo was widely published before the Brownsville trial and did much to gain sympathy for Margaret.

society, announced their support of her. When that happened, the Birth Control League, which had scorned Margaret such a short time before, quickly did an about-face.

The night of January 23, the evening before the trial was scheduled, a great dinner in honor of Margaret was held at the famous old Brevoort Hotel. Hundreds of people—society leaders, editors, and more than a few physicians—attended. The highlight of the dinner was Margaret's speech. She intended to present the same arguments to the judge and jury the following day.

Margaret went to court in a cheerful mood. Her remarks the night before had been well received by her influential audience. She was encouraged, too, when she saw the courtroom was packed; that there were hundreds of reporters and photographers on hand. These were her friends. It was a bitter disappointment, therefore, when one of the district attorneys asked for a postponement of another week. In spite of her protests, the judge agreed.

Tension built up again during the following week. Then, once more, the trial was postponed. Margaret waited as patiently as she could for the hearing the week after. That, too, was put off!

But support for Margaret was growing daily. Word came from Los Angeles that a birth-control league had been established there, too. *The Pictorial Review* reported that thousands of letters had been received after the article on birth control had appeared in the magazine the previous October. Ninety-seven per cent of those writing to the editor were heartily in favor of family planning.

Late in February, Margaret went to court for the final hearing of *The People v. Margaret Sanger*. She was confident now—almost cocky, as she waited her chance to speak.

It never came.

As soon as Judge Clayton banged his gavel, bringing the courtroom to order, one of the federal district attorneys arose. The federal government, he announced, wished to dismiss the charges against the defendant.

Judge Clayton banged his gavel again, and the case was closed. Margaret Sanger, "the frail little woman, the mother of a family," had chosen to fight the entire American government, and the government had backed away.

Chapter 8

THE FIRST CLINIC

MARGARET'S FRIENDS and supporters were jubilant. Those in the courtroom crowded around to congratulate her. Hundreds of others telephoned, while thousands wrote notes. But Margaret, relieved though she was that she need not go to jail, knew that her battle had barely begun.

It *was* a victory, she admitted. But it was a hollow one. Margaret's fondest hope was that the case would be heard and the judge convinced—and that he would then hand down a learned decision stating that birth control information was not obscene. Only then would she have the right to set up birth-control clinics like those in Holland; only then would doctors have the right to give American women the information and supplies that might well save their lives.

At the very least, Margaret had hoped to be allowed to speak, to plead for birth control. Her message would have been carried to women everywhere by the newspapers.

Since it hadn't been—well, why shouldn't Margaret carry it to them personally? Her trial had been front-page news throughout the country; her name was a household word, like that of a popular soap or cereal. Why not take advantage of all the publicity and arrange a speaking tour?

She immediately sent out thousands of letters, announcing, "I am touring to the western coast, starting April 1 . . ." They went to labor organizers, to Socialist, radical, and left-wing groups, to women who had shown an interest in birth control—to anyone who might help. Those who wished to sponsor lectures were invited to get in touch with Mrs. Sanger.

Dozens of them did. Margaret's mail was flooded with letters. Would she speak in Cleveland? Would she have time to go to Denver? Seattle?

Once Margaret had decided where she would go, she set to work on something equally important—what she would say. She carefully wrote out her speech, then climbed to the rooftop of her hotel. There, standing among the chimney pots and smokestacks, she repeated it again and again—and still again —to the laundry flapping on a line across the way.

Margaret began her speaking tour in New Rochelle. This time she would have a live audience, but her speech would be the one she had rehearsed.

All that day, before the meeting, Margaret quaked in fear. At the last moment she was certain she could not go through with the ordeal. Desperately, she looked for an excuse to avoid the meeting. She was suddenly taken ill, her car had broken down—anything, anything!

But too many women counted on her. Margaret knew that. She forgot about her excuses and concentrated on reaching New Rochelle on time. Then, taking a deep breath and praying inwardly that no one noticed her trembling, she marched onto the platform. In a quiet voice that was still filled with passion, she pleaded for the rights of women. She asked, as she would from coast to coast, that each one be allowed to choose for herself the size of her family.

Margaret was terrified before each lecture. Yet all went well until she reached Saint Louis. She was almost at ease that night as she drove to the Victoria Theater. Crowds had been enthusiastic everywhere. There had been ample publicity.

Then why was the Victoria dark, just fifteen minutes before the meeting was to begin? And why were all those people—Margaret later learned there were more than two thousand—milling around outside? The only way to find out was to ask someone.

"The theater's been barred," a man told Margaret. "We've been locked out." Why? "The Catholic Church doesn't approve of birth control."

But they had no right to interfere with the meeting! Moreover, they weren't going to stop Margaret! Hadn't she vowed to shout her message "from the housetops" if she had to?

She needn't go so far, now, though—nor so high, she thought with a smile. The back of an open car would do very nicely, instead.

Margaret stood in the back of the one she'd been riding in, and cupped her hands. Then she began her speech.

A policeman ran up to her at once. "You can't talk here," he barked.

Those in the crowd had other ideas, though. "Speech," they shouted. "Speech."

Margaret held up her hand for silence, then launched into the story of a woman who had visited her that very morning, begging for help. Again the police stopped her. At last Margaret gave up. It was useless even to try. But in a parting shot she called to the crowd, "This isn't Saint Louis. This is Czarist Russia."

Couldn't it have been Corning, New York, too—twenty-five years earlier? Margaret remembered the fierce pride of Michael Higgins, striding through the shower of fruit and vegetables, arm in arm with Colonel Ingersoll. Her own pride was just as great; her own resolve as firm. She was a Higgins, when all was said and done, and like a Higgins, she would fight back.

The next day she discovered that she had plenty of allies in Saint Louis. While many were not willing to stand up for birth control, they were more than glad to fight for free speech. They showed it, too, by inviting Margaret to address the luncheon of the Men's City Club, the next day. She did—and gained supporters among the most prominent people in the city. She already had all the newspapers on her side, and every one of them ran an editorial to protest the closing of the meeting at the Victoria.

After Saint Louis, Margaret went farther west—Denver, Los Angeles, Portland, Seattle. For three and a half months she traveled, speaking to one packed hall after another. Margaret was both exhausted and excited when she returned to New York. Interest in birth control was at fever pitch. In the wake of Margaret's tour birth-control leagues were set up in a dozen or more cities.

The time had come for a daring step. Margaret would set up a clinic. If it was closed by the police, which was certainly likely, she would have another chance to test the law. If it was not—well, all the better.

But where would the clinic be? And how would Margaret pay for it? It would cost far more than *The Woman Rebel* had.

As so often happened, both questions were answered by circumstances. One morning, a group of mothers from the Brownsville section of Brooklyn called on Margaret. Each had at least four children; none wanted more. They had come now to learn "the secret" of birth control.

Their pleas were so desperate, their stories so heartbreaking, that Margaret knew at once she must open her clinic in Brownsville. That settled, she sat down with paper and pencil to calculate expenses and to list friends who might contribute to them.

She had barely begun when the postman arrived with a batch of mail. In it was a letter from a supporter in California, enclosing a check for fifty dollars. Mrs. Sanger was to use it in any way she wanted to further the cause of birth control.

Margaret, waving the check in the air, rushed to show it to her sister, Ethel Byrne. "We have the rent!" she told her, a pleased smile lighting up her face. Confidently she added, "There'll be more."

Margaret was out early the next morning, tramping through the streets of Brownsville, looking for a few rooms that would do for the clinic. She didn't find them at once; it took weary days of searching before she came across just what she wanted. It was a small place, but large enough to be divided into the two rooms she needed. Margaret paid a month's rent, then went home and called a number of her friends.

They were all needed to help get the clinic ready, she explained. There was painting to be done, and scrubbing and cleaning, too.

Long before, Margaret had spoken of the clinic to two doctors, impressing them with its importance. Both had agreed to work there as soon as Margaret sent for them. Now, though, both found that they wouldn't have the time. They wished Margaret the best of luck, hoping she would understand.

Margaret did—only too well. Both doctors were afraid that if they worked with Margaret, they would lose the right to practice in accredited hospitals and might even lose their hard-won licenses.

Margaret looked around for other doctors. All were too busy, or had just made other plans, or even insisted they were not qualified for the work they would have to do.

Much as she wanted a doctor in charge, Margaret at last decided to open the clinic without one. It was better than delaying a month or so. Besides, both she and her sister, Ethel, were registered nurses. Since they had no alternative, the two would take charge of the medical side of the clinic.

She wrote to Fania Mindell, a social worker from Chicago, asking her to join the project. Fania promptly arrived in New York, ready to go to work. She was as enthusiastic as the others and spent much time, but very little money, buying curtains, desks, files, bookcases, and lamps for the offices.

Just before the clinic was to open, Margaret had flyers printed. They were in English, Yiddish, and Italian, the three languages spoken in the neighborhood. Addressed to "Mothers!" they asked:

> Can you afford to have a large family?
>
> If not, why do you have them?
>
> Safe, Harmless Information can be
> obtained of trained Nurses . . .

The address of the clinic followed.

When the flyers were ready, the three women went from one house to another, handing them out. They stuffed them into mailboxes, they climbed five or six flights of stairs to slip them under doors. When they found sympathetic shopkeepers, they left stacks with them.

The morning of October 16, 1916, the trio was up early and at the clinic before seven in the morning. There were still a few details to attend to, a few chores to be done, before the doors were opened for the first patients. Fania, giving a final swipe of the dustcloth, happened to glance out the window.

She gasped at what she saw! "Look!" she called to the others. "Just look!"

They hurried to the window, too. "Look!" Fania ordered again. A line of women, stretching halfway to the corner, waited for advice!

That day, at her desk in the front office, Fania took the histories of 140 of them. Then Margaret and Ethel, in the second room, explained birth control to seven or eight women at a time. Margaret had planned that later, when she had found a doctor, the women would be given individual advice. She even bought an examination table for the doctor's use.

For over a week Margaret and Ethel worked in the clinic. Each morning a long line of women appeared, waiting patiently to be let in. Often there were women still in line when the clinic closed.

Many of the neighbors were warm and friendly. The German baker down the street sent plates of doughnuts in to the three. Mrs. Rabinowitz, the wife of the landlord, brought down pots of fragrant, steaming tea. Even the mailman had a pleasant word and a big grin when he came.

All was going well. Margaret had held her breath at the beginning, but now everything was under control. If only she could find a doctor! When a friend gave her the name of one who might be willing to take on the task, she hurried off to see him, leaving Ethel and Fania in charge of the clinic.

That afternoon the women continued to stream in, as they had all week. Pathetic women with shawls on their heads, dressed in threadbare coats! Some brought children along, who waited with Fania in the outer room. Some came with their husbands. Sometimes a man shuffled in alone, to ask for help for his wife.

The contrast between them and a large, ruddy-faced woman who registered with the clinic immediately attracted Fania's attention. She was so much better dressed than the others. She was bold, whereas they were timid or frightened.

Fania listened skeptically to her story of a chronically ill husband who couldn't support their two children. When the woman insisted on paying two dollars, instead of the usual registration fee of ten cents, Fania was even more suspicious. She called Ethel aside and warned her that she was a policewoman. Still, Ethel insisted on seeing her and spoke to her freely.

The next day the waiting room was crowded when the same woman marched in. She went straight to Margaret. "I'm a policewoman," she snapped. "You're under arrest."

At that, three plainclothesmen from the vice squad appeared to arrest Fania, too. They lined up the women in the waiting room and took their names and addresses. The policewoman, Mrs. Whitehurst, not only seized the literature and the supplies on hand but took the clinical records of the patients as well.

Margaret promised the frightened women in the waiting

Margaret Sanger leaving Brooklyn Court of Special Sessions after her arraignment, October 1916.

room that they could leave in a few minutes. But the police guarded them for more than half an hour. At last they let the other women out and ordered Margaret and Fania to climb into the patrol wagon waiting outside.

Margaret was outraged by their behavior. What right had they to order her around that way! She would never ride with such brutes. Instead, she walked all the way to the station house, with an officer at her side.

Margaret was held in jail overnight, along with Fania and Ethel, who was arrested later. But the next afternoon she was back at the clinic in Brooklyn, carrying on as if nothing had happened.

A few days later, though, the clinic was closed again. This time it was for good.

Margaret was accused of "maintaining a public nuisance," and Mr. Rabinowitz, the landlord, was forced to evict her.

Chapter 9

PRISON

MARGARET HAD HOPED for a test case.
Now it seemed there were to be three of them.

She, Fania Mindell, and Ethel were all to be tried, but separately and on different charges. But it was Margaret who planned the defense of each.

Clearly, this was a situation different from the one Margaret had faced before. She could hardly hope to go in herself, without a lawyer, make her impassioned speech, and be set free. She could hardly ask that of the others, either. She needed a lawyer. Not only that, she needed a top-notch one.

She had heard of Jonah J. Goldstein. He was skilled in his

legal arguments, eloquent in court. He was sympathetic to birth
control, too—an important consideration. Even more important,
he had plenty of political connections. Goldstein was ideal.

Margaret went to see him soon after her arrest. She outlined
her plans to him. Before, she explained—as if he didn't know
—she wanted to prove that the law branding birth control obscene was wrong. Now she wanted to go much further. She
intended to do no less than prove that any law against birth
control was unconstitutional!

It was a tall order, as both Mr. Goldstein and Mrs. Sanger
knew. She could hardly count on such a decision from a lower
court, like that in Brooklyn, where the three were to be tried.
Jonah Goldstein thought the matter over, then told Margaret
quite frankly that she must be prepared to carry the case to the
Supreme Court.

Margaret made no objection. It would take money, of course,
but she would find it somewhere. She had always found the
money that was needed before, hadn't she?

It would be most helpful, Goldstein implied, if Margaret had
powerful friends.

But she did! The social leaders of New York—those who
had been at her side before her last trial—all stood behind her
now. They were women of wealth and position. Moreover, they
had both the time and the energy to devote to a fight. The most
prominent of them—those whose names were most often seen
in the society columns of the New York newspapers—immediately formed a Committee of 100 to support the accused women.

Many of them were in court that day, early in the new year
of 1917, when Ethel Byrne was brought to trial. She was the
last to be arrested; still, she was the first to appear before a
judge. The limousines of members of the committee blocked

the streets outside the courthouse; their chauffeurs waited, discussing the charges against Ethel, as well as the merits of birth control.

Margaret's star witness was a well-known doctor, Morris H. Kahn, who gave advice and supplies to women himself. After Ethel had testified, he would bolster her defense. But the court ruled he could not be sworn in; he was not acceptable as a witness.

As the women in the courtroom heard the refusal of the judge to admit the man's testimony, they muttered among themselves. But there was nothing they could do. They could do nothing, either, when Jonah Goldstein was allowed only fifteen minutes to sum up the defense plea. Most were furious, though. On the other hand, they nodded in approval when he asked that the case against Ethel be dismissed. The laws against birth control, he argued, deprived citizens of their liberty.

When Goldstein was overruled and Ethel found guilty, neither she nor Margaret was uneasy. The two of them had discussed the possibility of her being sent to jail. Yet they never believed such a thing could happen.

Two weeks later Ethel appeared before the court for sentencing. The room was crowded with beautifully dressed women, elegant in their furs and kid gloves. Some were married to judges; others to lawyers and bankers and wealthy merchants. Their very presence in court meant that Ethel would be let off with nothing more than a fine or a suspended sentence.

Ethel was almost as confident as Margaret had been when she appeared on trial. As they walked in together, Margaret pressed her sister's hand and whispered reassuringly, "There's nothing to worry about."

Ethel stood before the judge at the order of the bailiff. She

Ethel Byrne and Margaret Sanger in court, January 1917.

strained her ears to hear as he pronounced sentence. "Ethel Higgins Byrne . . ." the voice boomed, rich and full, ". . . thirty days . . ."

Ethel heard the words, but it was moments before she fully understood. At last the meaning was clear. Thirty days. Ethel drew herself up to her full height of five-foot-three and answered the judge. "I shall go on a hunger strike," she announced with dignity.

She was led off, handcuffed to an officer. She spent that night in the city jail. The next day she was transferred to the Work-house—the women's penitentiary on Blackwells Island, where she was to serve her time.

There were reporters waiting for her in the corridors. Ethel gave them the information they wanted; she had not yet eaten anything. She remembered that nourishment was sometimes slipped into drinking water and added, "I shan't drink any-thing, either."

Those were desperate days for the American nation and for the entire world. The war, which had broken out in 1914, had spread, becoming more and more bloody. Now America was on the verge of entering it. The papers were filled with stories of German offensives, of valiant stands against them.

But for days such stories were crowded off the front pages by the bulletins from the Workhouse. Little Ethel Byrne, re-fusing to eat as she sat in jail, was attracting as much attention as the Kaiser in Germany.

At first the prison officials pooh-poohed Ethel's defiance. Hadn't hundreds of other prisoners gone on hunger strikes? And hadn't they all come round after a short time?

But as Ethel went on with her hunger strike, they became alarmed. One morning a matron appeared, to let the smell of fresh-fried bacon and eggs drift into her cell. She coaxed Ethel to eat, promising, "No one will ever know."

Ethel turned away in disgust. "*I* would," she said.

For five days Ethel touched no food, no water. Then the prison doctor ordered her fed by force. It was the first time any woman in America had been so treated.

Then the warden ruled that no outsiders would be allowed to visit Ethel. He himself would issue reports on her health from time to time. At the moment, he said, Ethel Byrne was well and accepting the feedings "passively."

Margaret knew that wasn't so. If Ethel were well, she would be fighting furiously. Moreover, Margaret had secret sources of information within the prison. From them she learned that Ethel's sight was failing; that now her heart missed beats.

There was no time to be lost. Margaret called Mrs. Amos Pinchot, the head of her Committee of 100 and a personal friend of Charles Whitman, the governor of New York. The two drove at once to Albany to ask his help.

Governor Whitman was almost as outraged as they were. It was shocking, he said, banging his fist on the desk, that any woman be treated so brutally. He would see to it that she was pardoned at once. Of course, he added, Mrs. Byrne would agree not to give out that "forbidden information" in the future?

"I couldn't promise that," Margaret protested. "I'd have to ask Ethel, first."

Governor Whitman looked at her with genuine surprise. After a moment he dismissed Margaret and Mrs. Pinchot with a wave of his hand. He would like to help them, but what could he do? Especially when they were so unreasonable?

The two women hurried back to New York. There they found further reports about Ethel's pulse rate, her temperature. She was growing worse by the hour. At once, a delegation of prominent clubwomen was dispatched to Washington to plead with a group of senators.

The night before Margaret was to go on trial, there was a huge rally in support of poor Ethel. It was held at New York's famous Carnegie Hall—with seats for thousands—and it was jammed.

Margaret spent the next day in court, listening to legal arguments which she didn't understand in the least. When court was adjourned, she rushed to Blackwells Island with Mrs. Pinchot.

Ethel's condition was serious by now—close to critical. For the first time Margaret was permitted to see her.

Ethel lay on a cot in her cell, too weak to move. After so long without food or water, she was delirious. Margaret, fearing Ethel would die, wired Governor Whitman that she, on Ethel's behalf, accepted his terms for a pardon. Shortly later, she learned that he had already granted it.

Mrs. Pinchot's car was waiting. Margaret herself moved Ethel to it on a stretcher. An ambulance was summoned to meet the car in New York, and Ethel was taken to Margaret's apartment.

For two weeks she hovered between life and death. It was a full year before she recovered from her ordeal.

Meanwhile, Margaret's trial went on. The women who had been at the clinic at the time Margaret was arrested were called as witnesses. Eager to help, they praised her and her work, never realizing that nothing could be worse—that they were proving her guilt. But Margaret's lawyer managed to arouse the sympathy of everyone, including the judges, by questioning the women on their own backgrounds of poverty and illness.

For the most part, though, the proceedings consisted of dull and dry legal arguments. Using such tactics, Goldstein had prevailed upon the courts merely to fine Fania Mindell fifty dollars. (Later, that decision was reversed.) But Fania, whose case had been heard before Margaret's, was only accused of giving out a copy of one of Margaret's pamphlets, "What Every Girl Should Know." The one question before the court was whether or not that booklet was "indecent."

Margaret, though, faced far more serious charges than either Ethel or Fania had. It was she, after all, who had written "What Every Girl Should Know." It was she who had opened the clinic and asked Ethel to assist her. And, of course, like Ethel, she had instructed the women of Brownsville in the use of contraceptives.

Each day Margaret went to court, her friends and allies went, too. Each day, they presented Margaret with an armful of long-stemmed red roses. As she sat there, the flowers in her arms, "she looked more like the guest of honor at a reception," said a reporter, "than the defendant in a criminal trial."

But trial it was, and Jonah Goldstein droned on and on, dredging up obscure, almost unheard of laws, or shouted his objection to evidence about to be admitted, or to some question asked.

Since Goldstein knew he could never convince the court that Margaret was not guilty, he made no effort to do so. Instead, he made it clear that he planned to take the case to the Supreme Court. He was sure the nine wise old men of the nation's highest court would see things in a different light. They would reinterpret the law and thereby change it. If this was so, wouldn't it be absurd for the present court to impose any sentence on Margaret, let alone a harsh one?

The three men sitting in judgment on Margaret at the moment, though, had other ideas. Why should they let her go free now? Wouldn't she simply open another clinic and violate the law again?

Margaret's attitude was simply "I will not compromise. I am right. The law is wrong. The law must be changed."

Knowing this, Goldstein did his best to keep Margaret from testifying. But he was no match for her. As he summed up his plea, he stepped in front of her, speaking directly to the bench in a low voice, hoping Margaret would not hear.

But she caught his words. "My client promises not to violate the law." Margaret, standing now, tugged on his coat for attention. Goldstein shifted this way and that, trying to hide Margaret from the bench. At last one of the judges prodded Goldstein with "Your client wishes to speak to you, Counselor."

Margaret was called to the stand at last and took the oath. For twenty minutes, the panel argued with her. They were prepared to "consider extreme clemency," they said. Did Margaret know what that meant?

Yes. It meant no more than a suspended sentence.

However, Margaret must respect the law if "extreme clemency" were shown.

"I cannot respect the law as it stands today," Margaret said quietly.

The three judges put their heads together for a brief, whispered conference. Then, with a bang of his gavel, one announced: "It is the judgment of this court that you be confined to the Workhouse for thirty days."

There was a moment of stunned silence in the courtroom.

Then, from the back, came the voice of one lone woman. "Shame!"

Chapter **1O**

THE LAW IS WRONG!

IKE ETHEL, Margaret was taken to Blackwells Island to
serve her jail term. She decided at once that another
hunger strike was useless and dropped any notion of it.

Not that she was a model prisoner! Far from it! To begin
with, she refused to be fingerprinted. Then she wouldn't sub-
mit to the customary medical examination. There was a short
struggle, with Margaret holding her own against the authorities. Soon they had had enough—of both Higgins sisters. They
managed to wash their hands of Margaret by transferring her
to the Queens County Penitentiary.

Margaret followed the rules when she had to—or when she

wanted to. Anyway, because she was again fighting tuberculosis, she was given special privileges. Instead of working in the laundry or the sewing room, she stayed in her cell and wrote; instead of eating dry bread and drinking bitter tea, like the others, she had crackers and milk.

Margaret, of course, attracted a great deal of attention. The other inmates all seemed to have heard of her, and most knew of Ethel's hunger strike. But they were no more interested in Margaret than she was in them. Where did they come from? What kind of life had led them to prison? Above all, how many brothers and sisters did each have? Margaret set about finding out and ended up asking permission to instruct the woman in birth-control techniques! It was never given, of course, but the officials looked the other way when Margaret went ahead with some informal talks.

Most of her time, though, was spent in planning for the future. What should be the next step in bringing birth control to the women who wanted it?

So far, most of Margaret's success had come from stirring up trouble. It had certainly gained attention, even though it had landed her in jail.

But now she must find some other way to move forward. People had noticed Margaret. Since they had, she would educate them, teaching them the hows and the whys of birth control.

She would need a vast organization for that. But it would serve a second purpose, too. It could spearhead a movement for new legislation. Once the laws Margaret had in mind were passed, no woman need languish in prison for the reasons she now did.

Margaret was no sooner released—after an even more furious battle against fingerprinting than before—than she was back in the thick of the fighting. She dared not open another clinic, of course. But she could advance on other fronts.

As usual, there was stiff opposition. And, as usual, Margaret thrived on it. The very day she left prison there was a new skirmish in her war against what was considered "nice."

This time a welcome-home celebration had been arranged in her honor, at Delmonico's Hotel, one of those most popular with New York's social leaders. The contract was signed, and the room paid for. But a phone call, at almost the last minute, let the sponsors know that "unfortunately" it would not be available. They hurried around, looking for another place. Everywhere they went they heard the same thing when they mentioned Margaret. "We're very sorry . . ."

Margaret, though, had no such problem. She marched into the Plaza Hotel, the most elegant in all the city, and asked for a banquet hall for that evening. She got the hall at once, as well as dozens of newspaper stories!

She went on speaking tours. She wrote countless articles. Then, that year, 1917, she took two new and important steps to reach the public. The first was to make a propaganda movie, unheard-of at the time. It was called *The Hand That Rocks the Cradle*, and it starred Margaret. A short while later she founded a new magazine, *The Birth Control Review*.

The Hand That Rocks the Cradle was quickly suppressed. But *The Birth Control Review* fared better. It was more scientific than *The Woman Rebel*, since Margaret no longer either wanted or needed to shock readers. Instead of her own fiery prose, she filled its pages with scholarly words of authorities like Havelock Ellis, and reasoned pleas by H. G. Wells.

It was a difficult time. There was never money in the till, although there were plenty of people who pulled out their

—Sophia Smith Collection, Smith College

Margaret Sanger on one of her many lecture tours.

pocketbooks when Margaret asked. But that money was always earmarked for paper or printing or postage. Margaret refused to use any for herself.

Her own income from her writing and speeches was so small that she had a hard time scraping together enough money for a dress when she was to lecture. But her wealthy friends usually came to the rescue. "Not a thing to wear? Here, Margaret, take this. It's just your size." After the lecture it would be, "But keep it, Margaret. It's so becoming on you." Which was hardly surprising, since the outfit had been bought with Margaret in mind.

Margaret's poverty was a hardship, but it was bearable. But how much worse it was to be separated from Stuart and Grant!

She had sent the boys to boarding school, knowing how they felt—and would feel—about coming home to an empty house every day, or one presided over by a housekeeper or maid. Bill had agreed that this was the best solution. So had Margaret's sisters, Mary and Nan. All three had been able to scrape together the money for a large share of the boys' expenses. Before long, Stuart was able to earn part, too.

Bill was as devoted to Margaret as ever. He longed to take up their life together, again. But Margaret had no time for marriage. With real regret she explained to Bill that her work came—and must come—first.

Bill wasn't the only man who found Margaret enchanting. She was still young, still slender. Her hair was as red as it had ever been—and her temper as sharp! When Havelock Ellis heard Margaret described as that "shining and gentle woman," his eyes twinkled with laughter, making him look like Santa. "Is he aware," he asked, "that the 'gentle woman' has sometimes to be held back from deeds of violence by men in khaki?"

Ellis admired Margaret tremendously, as she did him. H. G.

Wells and a dozen other men were captivated by her. But Margaret was too busy with her work, with the cause she was fighting for, to settle down anywhere or with anyone.

For a long time she had worked at home, either in a bedroom, the dining room, or a corner of the kitchen of the apartment she kept when her sons were home. When they left for boarding school, she moved into a studio in the section of New York known as Chelsea.

It was the least expensive place she could find. For forty dollars a month, Margaret rented a good-sized room at the back of a tumbledown building. There was no elevator. The stairs that Margaret and her visitors climbed to the fourth floor had broken treads. The halls they passed through were dark, with cracked and peeling plaster. At least once, Margaret found a dead rat almost at her door.

Margaret did her best to make her quarters cheerful. She hung yellow curtains at the window and tossed bright cushions on the couch. Even so, it was dingy. With all her books and papers, it was crowded, too.

When Dr. Frederick Blossom arrived from Cleveland to fight beside Margaret, he took one look around her apartment and decided it would never do. A few weeks later they were sharing a two-room office near the lower end of Fifth Avenue, the first real office Margaret had ever had. On the door were the neatly lettered words "Birth Control."

Margaret had one room to herself. It was small, but there was space for her files and a large desk, which was littered with the thousands of letters that poured in each week.

Dr. Blossom worked as hard and as long as Margaret did. He often stayed in the office until midnight. He seldom even went out for meals, eating an apple at his desk for lunch, having coffee and a sandwich sent in for dinner. He had as much time to contribute to birth control as Margaret, as well as a great deal more money, and he was generous with both.

Besides, Dr. Blossom had a talent—a genius, even—for taking charge and making things work. He had raised money for other worthy causes; now he dunned his friends for sizable contributions.

His mere presence in the movement—and in the office—brought in willing and efficient volunteers, who took over the details of the clerical work and kept the office running. Dr. Blossom, meanwhile, developed a system for classifying mail, so that all letters could be answered. Even with dozens of volunteers, it would have been out of the question otherwise.

He organized the rallies and meetings for birth control, seeing to it that halls were hired and speakers reminded of the day and hour. He sent followers to Albany, the capital of New York State, to lobby for birth-control bills. Above all, he organized the New York State Birth Control League, the most powerful such group yet to be formed.

Most of its members were Socialists, like Margaret. Like her, they traditionally opposed war. But those were the dark days when it seemed that German troops might overrun the entire free world. Faced with such a threat, many Socialists urged that American troops be sent into battle. Dr. Blossom was one of those who firmly believed that the time had come to fight.

Margaret, though, clung to the views she had always held. It would be sheer folly, she insisted, for the country to take up arms against the Kaiser, no matter what the circumstances.

The two argued the subject with increasing bitterness. Finally Margaret goaded Dr. Blossom beyond endurance by printing an editorial against American entry into the war, in *The Birth Control Review* for June, 1917.

Furious, he said no more about it. Instead he took action—

and when Margaret arrived at the office one morning, she found it stripped bare.

Desks, chairs, and filing cabinets had been carried away. All of Margaret's important papers—the records of patients, the case histories, the list of subscribers to *The Birth Control Review*—were gone. Everything—*everything!* Only the telephone had been left behind, set on a packing box now.

When Margaret's secretary arrived a few minutes later, she was as shocked as Margaret. But there was no use crying over spilled milk, or stolen furniture, either. Instead, the two women pooled the contents of their purses, then headed for the nearest second-hand furniture shop. For less than twenty dollars they were able to buy enough to make the office at least usable.

Margaret hurried back to her office and used the telephone so conveniently left behind to call her lawyer. He was to bring charges against Dr. Blossom, she ordered. Further, she would sue for the return of her papers and her files.

She never got them back. But for four years the feud between Margaret and Dr. Blossom continued, with each hurling charges at the other regularly. Even after that, Margaret never forgave Dr. Blossom while he, in turn, let everyone know what he thought of Mrs. Sanger.

Margaret already had a heavy load to carry. The battle with Dr. Blossom added to her problems. The flow of funds from wealthy patrons slowed, then almost stopped. Once again, Margaret lived from hand to mouth, borrowing even from her sisters to pay the printer when he refused to wait longer, begging the few dollars she needed for the rent, saving money for stamps by skimping on her own food.

There were times when Margaret felt she could not carry on the struggle. It was too difficult! If only she could disappear!

Go away! Leave it to others! But there were always three or four of the faithful to bolster her spirits. Even when news came that her conviction had been sustained by the courts on her first appeal, they managed to cheer her up. Her lawyer would merely carry the case higher, they assured her.

Jonah Goldstein did, and the case was reviewed by the New York Court of Appeals, the highest in the state. On January 8, 1918, Judge Frederick Crane made his decision known. The lower courts were right, he said. Mrs. Sanger most certainly broke the law by giving women advice on birth control. There was no doubt, either, that the law was constitutional.

She had violated another section of the penal code as well, since doctors—and doctors alone—were allowed to instruct women on the means of contraception. Furthermore, doctors had that right only when it was necessary to prevent or cure disease.

But what, Margaret wondered, did Judge Crane mean by "disease"? The future of birth control hung on that.

She quickly read the rest of what he had written: " 'Disease', by Webster's International Dictionary, is defined to be 'an alteration in the state of the body, or of some of its organs . . . causing or threatening pain or sickness.' "

Margaret read the decision again, more carefully this time. Did she dare believe it?

Judge Crane's definition of disease was not limited to any specific illness, as earlier ones had been. It was broad enough to permit doctors to give advice to women everywhere.

Margaret was guilty, yes. But birth control was legal!

There was nothing, now, that could hold Margaret back.

Chapter 11

THE MOVEMENT GROWS

THERE WERE NEW CONVERTS to be made. Margaret went out to preach to them, wherever they were—below the Mason-Dixon line, in the Midwest, on the Pacific Coast. Wherever she could be heard, Margaret went.

There were books to be written.

Margaret settled Stuart in his boarding school for another year. Then, with Grant in tow, she hurried off to California to write *Woman and the New Race*. It was the first of a half dozen she would publish.

There was research to be done.

As early as 1915, Havelock Ellis told Margaret of a remarkable new contraceptive. It was in the form of a chemical, developed in Germany.

Because of the war, Margaret could do nothing about obtaining the German chemical at the time. Now, though, she trotted off to find it. She found it, too, after a search that led from one German city to another. The product had its drawbacks: it was too expensive for general use, too difficult to make. But American companies modified the formula to make a safer and more effective contraceptive.

Margaret went to England where she was wined and dined by friends and whisked off to the countryside each weekend. The rest of the time, she worked as even she had never done before.

She visited clinics; there were already two in England, and both were flourishing. She met with doctors and lawyers and sociologists, arguing and pleading with them, charming them and winning them to the ranks of her supporters.

Public speaking exhausted her, and for a while she turned down all engagements. But the British people wanted to hear Margaret. At last she gave in and went on tour, giving thirty lectures in England and Scotland.

Back in London, she took up her round of conferences and meetings. She was there when word came from New York, telling her she had been granted a divorce from Bill. She had brought the suit against him, with his agreement, although they were still the best of friends. At long last, both had realized that their lives were too different, their paths too separate, to continue together.

By December 1920, Margaret was in New York again, with

a new scheme. Since it was legal for doctors to give birth-control advice, she would insist that they do so—and in New York hospitals.

She got in touch with a friend, Juliet Rublee, and the two sent a number of desperately sick women to ask for contraceptives. Even though all risked their lives by having children, all were refused help.

Then Juliet, the wife of a wealthy lawyer and a noted hostess, began inviting the most distinguished doctors in the city to her home for dinner. As the salad was being served, she steered the conversation around to birth control. At dessert time—just as, without fail, one of the guests attacked Margaret as a "wild-eyed radical" or railed against her "loose morals"—the door would open, and in would come a demure Margaret.

She always wore a simple black dress. "The more outrageous your ideas," she insisted, "the more conservative your clothes must be."

Conservative, yes. But also becoming. Margaret always managed to look radiantly beautiful. Usually, too, she managed to sway people to her side.

That was a frantic winter and spring. Margaret was looking ahead to the First International Conference on Birth Control. As yet, it was just a dream. It could only come true if Margaret went to England again to round up both speakers and backers.

Besides, she was planning a second clinic. This time, there would definitely be a doctor in charge. There would also be a marriage counselor on hand, as well as a psychiatrist. Pregnant women could come for prenatal care; those who had children could leave them in the nursery while they consulted doctors. Research would be carried on, too, both on contraception and on ways of preventing sterility; help would be given both to those women who wanted to limit their families and to those who wanted children but had not been able to have them.

Margaret found a building near the Lower East Side, a near-perfect location for a clinic. She leased a few rooms, where a dentist had once had his offices, and hoped to open the clinic the following year.

She was short of cash—nothing new—and overburdened with work. She continued her lecture tours. She edited *The Birth Control Review*. She took charge of all the details of the projects planned.

Her tiny office was hardly luxurious. Margaret still used the second-hand furniture she had bought to replace the desk and chairs Dr. Blossom had taken, years before. But now, day after day, there were vases of fresh, long-stemmed American Beauty roses on her desk.

They came from J. Noah H. Slee, the prosperous president of the Three-in-One Oil Company. He had been taken, over his strong objections, to hear Margaret speak a few months before. Birth control, after all, was not a subject to appeal to a man with his proper South African upbringing. Yet Margaret, looking feminine and fragile, intrigued him more than any woman he had known.

At first he was content to send her flowers. Then he managed to turn up wherever she might be. When she went to London that summer, he was in The Hague on business and offered to fly to London to see her, a very new means of traveling and, according to Margaret, "the fashion now."

Yet Margaret scarcely had time for anyone. The conference was to open in New York on November 11, 1921. An important meeting would be held at Town Hall, where a panel of medical, legal, and religious experts would discuss the question "Birth

Control: Is it Moral?" Margaret lined up speakers in England before she sailed for home.

She drove to the meeting with a British Member of Parliament who was to address the group. As they neared Town Hall, they were amazed to see the huge throng outside. Margaret expected an overflow crowd, but were *all* those people being turned away?

She pushed her way through the crowd to the door of the hall. There, a burly policeman stopped her, bawling, "You can't go in."

"Why not? I'm one of the speakers at the meeting."

"Lady," the officer said, "there ain't gonna be no meeting."

Margaret hurried across the street to call police headquarters. Why had the meeting been banned?

When the police insisted they didn't know, Margaret put in a call to the mayor. Then she saw that a policeman was letting people out of the hall. She could slip in when they opened the door!

She ducked under a blue-sleeved arm. Inside, people stood in the aisles, confused and angry. Margaret hastened to the footlights where a man lifted her up and almost flung her on the stage. As Margaret caught her balance, he leaped to the platform himself. Nearby a bewildered usher stared in amazement as he waited to present Margaret with an armful of roses sent by an admirer.

The man seized the flowers and handed them to Margaret. "Mrs. Sanger's here," he shouted. "Mrs. Sanger's here!"

Margaret called "Don't leave," and a wave of applause swept the hall. Since standing in the aisle created a fire hazard—and a valid reason to close the hall—she ordered everyone back to his seat.

She soon learned what had happened. A man had appeared, escorted by a police captain, to say there could be no meeting because "an indecent, immoral subject is to be discussed." A few questions, and he admitted that he was Monsignor Dineen, the secretary of the Archbishop of New York.

The Catholic Church! It might be Saint Louis—or Corning —all over again. But it needn't be if Margaret took it to court!

To do so, she must be arrested. Well, that was easy enough! She beckoned to others on the platform, told them what she intended to do, and what *they* must do. Then she stepped forward and began her speech.

At once a blue-coated officer shoved her aside. "Be quiet!" he ordered.

Margaret began again. Again the officer shoved her aside. Someone else tried to speak. When the police interfered, a third stepped forward to address the audience.

There had been confusion in the hall before. Now there was chaos.

More police were called. A squad crowded onto the platform, pushing speakers and committee members to their seats. Another squad rushed up and down the aisles, trying to make the audience leave.

Margaret looked around and saw Monsignor Dineen signaling the police from the wings. Finally he whispered a command and an officer strode up to Margaret. "You're under arrest," he announced.

Then one woman after another rose, began to speak, and was promptly arrested. At last they were herded outside to a waiting police van. When they refused to get in, they were marched through the streets to the station house, followed by thousands of cheering supporters.

—*Sophia Smith Collection, Smith College*

Pearl Buck (left) presented the Town Hall Club medal to Margaret Sanger in 1937.

At a hearing the next day, the case was dismissed. Margaret had violated no law; the police had no evidence to present.

This time the Catholic Church had bungled badly in taking on the daughter of Michael Higgins. The issue was not a moral one now. It was a matter of freedom of speech.

Every newspaper in New York understood that. Every one supported Margaret and attacked the Church. Scores of others throughout the country did the same.

Hundreds of thousands rallied to Margaret's cause, and the birth-control movement shot ahead. Margaret, to her surprise, was being hailed as a heroine.

Her reputation grew, through the years, until, in 1937, she was awarded the annual medal of the Town Hall Club. Pearl Buck, the novelist who had already won the Pulitzer Prize and who would win the Nobel Prize in literature the following year, pinned the decoration on Margaret's dress.

It was for "the most conspicuous contribution of the year— 1936—to the enrichment of life." And it was given to Margaret on the platform of Town Hall itself, where she had been arrested just sixteen years earlier for trying to discuss the subject of birth control.

Margaret stepped forward, wearing the gleaming bit of gold, and finished the speech the police had interrupted.

Chapter 12

THE LAST YEARS

URING THOSE SIXTEEN YEARS between her arrest and her award, much had happened.

Just a year after she was arrested on the platform of Town Hall, Margaret was invited to visit Japan, where overpopulation was a critical problem. With fourteen-year-old Grant at her side, she sailed for the Orient. When her ship berthed in Honolulu, she was acclaimed, like a movie star or a champion prizefighter, by a solid mass of people on the shore.

Her reception was the same in Japan and Korea. Both governments frowned on her visits, but permitted them because of the clamor of the public.

From Korea, Margaret went most of the way around the

world. Hong Kong was first, then Singapore, Cairo, and finally London.

Noah Slee, like Margaret, was on board the *Taiyo Maru* when it sailed from San Francisco for Tokyo. He insisted this was a business trip. It was strange, though, that his business carried him wherever Margaret went. Since he was along, why should a fragile, helpless woman like Margaret have to ship her luggage or buy her tickets? he asked. The capable Mr. Slee was most willing to do it for her.

By the time the three had traveled up the Nile, Grant had had enough of "being dragged at the tail end of a typhoon." Being with Mother was exhausting. He came down with a virus infection, and Slee took him to Switzerland to recover. Then, to Grant's delight, he was packed off to a summer camp at home.

Slee caught up with Margaret in London, where she was organizing another international conference. For three years the staid businessman had been her slave. He showered her with gifts. Many were personal, but he also paid the printer, sent the monthly check to the landlord, and bought supplies.

He had reorganized Margaret's New York office, too. He'd been shocked at her inefficiency—the woman hadn't the foggiest notion of how to file papers! She didn't even have postage meters or scales! Soon Slee had the place running as smoothly as if it were oiled with Three-in-One.

At last, in London, during the summer of 1922, Margaret agreed to become Mrs. J. Noah H. Slee. She made it plain, though, that she would live her own life. She would be known as Mrs. Slee on social occasions; otherwise she would be called "Margaret Sanger." She would go on with her work. She would . . . She gave J. Noah a list of conditions. Once such matters were settled, they were married by a justice of the peace.

A honeymoon? There was no time! Margaret hurried off to

New York to set up the new birth-control clinic, while J. Noah went to Fishkill, some sixty miles from the city. There he supervised the building of Willow Lake, the luxurious home that was his wedding gift to Margaret.

The new clinic was opened in January 1923. Dr. Hannah Stone headed the medical staff. Margaret warned her that she faced jail for it, despite the court ruling on birth control. Dr. Stone was hardly surprised; she had already been forced to give up her hospital post for joining Margaret.

Others opposed clinics, too. Even the members of the Birth Control League could not see that only doctors should give advice. They still saw birth control as a matter of free speech, rather than a medical problem.

Yet Margaret went ahead. In almost no time, her little clinic was too small for the hordes of women who turned up. A new and larger one had to be opened.

Soon there were others across the country. Chicago, Baltimore, Detroit, all had them. By 1930, there were fifty-five birth-control clinics in America, with a dozen others sprinkled throughout the world.

Birth control led to healthier, happier families. Margaret saw that it could also help nations to become prosperous and thus even aid in the cause of world peace. Accordingly, she suggested a Conference on World Population to the Birth Control League.

The members of the league immediately raised objections. Where, they demanded, would the money come from? It was the usual question; Margaret ignored it and organized the conference alone.

Alone, that is, except for Noah Slee. He had retired and could be at Margaret's side constantly. They worked together for two solid years, raising money, persuading scientists to attend, hiring secretaries and interpreters and arranging for accommodations.

Sir Bernard Mallet, a distinguished Englishman, served as chairman. Margaret had confidence in him and in the outstanding speakers they had chosen together. But the night before the conference opened, in Geneva, in 1927, Margaret was crushed to learn that it had been taken out of her hands. Birth control was not to be mentioned. Her connection with the conference was not to be known!

The Italian dictator Benito Mussolini had brought pressure to bear on Sir Bernard to invite his own spokesman, Corrado Gini. When Sir Bernard gave in to Mussolini, who was clamoring for more children to man a future army, the Spanish government demanded that *their* representative attend. Then the Belgians and a reactionary French group insisted on choosing delegates.

All were opponents of birth control, who immediately set about turning the conference into a propaganda exercise in favor of large families! But the scientists Margaret herself had invited managed to make their voices heard. As a result, the conference became one of her greatest triumphs.

She headed for home, after a brief rest and a strenuous lecture tour, and found more trouble brewing. Newcomers had been added to the directors of the Birth Control League, and they seemed more interested in balancing the budget than in expanding birth control. Margaret was no longer even welcome at league headquarters.

So, with a few women who had been at her side since the beginning, she resigned. But she refused to hand over control of the clinic. With Slee's moral and financial support, she kept it going and growing.

Margaret had more—but not much more—time to spend with

her family now. Her father had died, when he was well past eighty, the year before. She missed him, of course, but was happy that she, with Noah's help, had been able to buy a house for him in Truro. She was pleased, too, that Ethel could live in it now.

Willow Lake was finished and staffed with servants. Margaret escaped to it often. Grant was doing well as a doctor, and Stuart, although older, had begun to study medicine after a few years as a stock broker.

Stuart, though, was not well. He had suffered from a sinus infection since he was a small child. It was worse now, and Margaret spent much of her time nursing him.

It was just then that word came from the clinic of another raid. Margaret left Stuart and hurried down. At the clinic, she found that the police had swooped down, arrested doctors and nurses, and taken the names of the waiting women. Moreover, they seized records so confidential that even nurses never saw them.

Once again, Margaret was arrested. But there was never a question of her going to jail. Birth control was now legal and even acceptable. It was soon learned that the raid had been ordered by a public official involved in a local scandal, who hoped to divert attention from his role in it. Scorn was generally heaped on him, while Margaret was defended. The public was especially incensed that the files had been taken, and medical societies and a number of law associations lodged strong protests with the police.

As before, such tactics proved a boon to the birth-control movement, bringing in more and more supporters. Even the Birth Control League quickly offered to join hands with Margaret.

But she preferred to go her own way, and that way led her around the world again and again in the following years. Russia,

India, where she conferred with Mahatma Gandhi, China—
wherever there was a problem of overpopulation, Margaret was
to be found.

She still controlled her clinic; now she set up her own organization, devoted to education on family limitation. With its
backing, she worked for close to two years in Washington,
lobbying for a bill to make it easier for doctors to obtain contraceptive information and supplies. Such a bill was never
passed, but in 1936 the federal courts ruled that such supplies
could be imported from other countries, as well as shipped from
one state to another. The decision was as great a victory as that
making birth control legal.

During those years, Margaret had her share of misfortune.
Stuart was still ill and showed no improvement, in spite of nine
operations. Finally Margaret rebelled against such treatment
—and his doctors—and hustled him off to Tucson, Arizona.
There, in the warm sun, Stuart began to recover. J. Noah soon
joined Margaret there. Her own health was failing; his was
none too good. But they were at least together, relaxing, as they
never had before.

It wasn't long before Grant, with his wife, took a house
nearby. Then, as the years passed, there were grandchildren,
to Margaret's unending delight.

There was plenty of social life in Tucson, and Margaret enjoyed it thoroughly. Friends visited from afar, as well. But her
oldest and dearest ones were gone. Havelock Ellis, who had
shared her ideas so completely and had been closer to her than
any other person, died in London in 1939. Eighteen months
later, J. Noah suffered a series of strokes. Margaret cared for
him during his illness. Then he, too, was gone.

Margaret lived on in Tucson, continuing with her work as
long as she could. In 1942 the Birth Control League was united

Margaret Sanger after receiving an honorary LL.D. from Smith College, June 1949.

with Margaret's Education Department, to form the Planned Parenthood Federation of America, with Margaret as honorary chairman.

She continued to travel. Sometimes it was in her own country. When help was needed in the dust bowl of Oklahoma or in the migrant camps of California, Margaret went. When the Second World War was over, she went to England again. Then there were trips to the Scandinavian countries. Conferences were held there and throughout the world; Margaret appeared wherever they might be.

But during the last ten years of her life, Margaret was almost an invalid. As she had grown older, the world began to shower her with awards. In 1949 she was given an honorary Doctor of Laws degree from Smith College. Others followed, and in 1960 her name was proposed for the Nobel Peace Prize.

Margaret Higgins Sanger died, in Tucson, on September 6, 1966. But her work goes on. The movement started by a red-haired "woman rebel" at her own dining-room table is now worldwide.

Governments everywhere have seen the need for population control and are setting aside funds both to carry on research and to teach women how to use contraceptives. The United States is in the forefront of the fight. Two former presidents, Dwight D. Eisenhower and Harry S Truman, served as co-chairmen of the Planned Parenthood Federation. Another, Lyndon B. Johnson, accepted the Margaret Sanger Award for his aid to the cause of birth control.

Each, of course, was the head of the very government that had sent Margaret Sanger to prison for preaching and teaching birth control, less than fifty years ago.

INDEX